MW01232562

Microsoft® Office Project 2007

Level 1

Microsoft® Office Project 2007: Level 1

Part Number: 084774
Course Edition: 1.1

NOTICES

DISCLAIMER: While Element K Corporation takes care to ensure the accuracy and quality of these materials, we cannot guarantee their accuracy, and all materials are provided without any warranty whatsoever, including, but not limited to, the implied warranties of merchantability or fitness for a particular purpose. The name used in the data files for this course is that of a fictitious company. Any resemblance to current or future companies is purely coincidental. We do not believe we have used anyone's name in creating this course, but if we have, please notify us and we will change the name in the next revision of the course. Element K is an independent provider of integrated training solutions for individuals, businesses, educational institutions, and government agencies. Use of screenshots, photographs of another entity's products, or another entity's product name or service in this book is for editorial purposes only. No such use should be construed to imply sponsorship or endorsement of the book by, nor any affiliation of such entity with Element K. This courseware may contain links to sites on the Internet that are owned and operated by third parties (the "External Sites"). Element K is not responsible for the availability of, or the content located on or through, any External Site. Please contact Element K if you have any concerns regarding such links or External Sites.

TRADEMARK NOTICES Element K and the Element K logo are trademarks of Element K Corporation and its affiliates.

Microsoft® Office Project Professional 2007 is a registered trademark of Microsoft Corporation in the U.S. and other countries; the Microsoft products and services discussed or described may be trademarks of Microsoft Corporation. All other product names and services used throughout this course may be common law or registered trademarks of their respective proprietors.

Copyright © 2007 Element K Corporation. All rights reserved. Screenshots used for illustrative purposes are the property of the software proprietor. This publication, or any part thereof, may not be reproduced or transmitted in any form or by any means, electronic or mechanical, including photocopying, recording, storage in an information retrieval system, or otherwise, without express written permission of Element K, 500 Canal View Boulevard, Rochester, NY 14623, (585) 240-7500, (800) 478-7788. Element K Courseware's World Wide Web site is located at **www.elementkcourseware.com**.

This book conveys no rights in the software or other products about which it was written; all use or licensing of such software or other products is the responsibility of the user according to terms and conditions of the owner. Do not make illegal copies of books or software. If you believe that this book, related materials, or any other Element K materials are being reproduced or transmitted without permission, please call (800) 478-7788.

HELP US IMPROVE OUR COURSEWARE

Your comments are important to us. Please contact us at Element K Press LLC, 1-800-478-7788, 500 Canal View Boulevard, Rochester, NY 14623, Attention: Product Planning, or through our Web site at **http://support.elementkcourseware.com**.

Microsoft® Office Project 2007: Level 1

Lesson 5: Finalizing the Project Plan

About This Course

You need to gather information about the various tasks involved, resources required to accomplish the tasks, and the overall cost in order to plan a project. Microsoft® Office Project Professional 2007 acts as a tool that assists you in managing your projects. In this course, you will create and modify a project plan.

Regardless of job title, most of us have, at one time or another, played the role of project manager. If you have ever been responsible for coordinating a variety of tasks that had to be completed within a specific time frame for a set amount of money, you have acted as a project manager. You also know, then, that keeping track of all of the project details, like tasks, resources, and costs, while continuing to focus on the project goals, can be quite a challenge. Whether you are a trained Project Management Professional (PMP), a resource manager, or a team member, Microsoft® Office Project 2007 can assist you in managing your projects by storing project information, calculating and maintaining the project schedule, tracking project costs, and analyzing and communicating project data.

Course Description

Target Student

This course is designed for a person who has an understanding of project management concepts, who is responsible for creating and modifying project plans, and who needs a tool to manage these project plans.

Course Prerequisites

Students enrolled for this course should have the following:

■ An understanding of project management concepts.

■ Knowledge of a Windows operating system, either Windows XP or Windows Vista.

The following would be helpful, but are not required:

■ Project Management Fundamentals Part 1 and 2 (Element K course).

■ Harvard Manage Mentor: Project Management (Element K course).

■ A basic knowledge of Microsoft Word and Microsoft Excel.

How to Use This Book

As a Learning Guide

Each lesson covers one broad topic or a set of related topics. Lessons are arranged in the order of increasing proficiency with *Microsoft® Project 2007*; skills you acquire in one lesson are used and developed in subsequent lessons. For this reason, you should work through the lessons in sequence.

We have organized each lesson into results-oriented topics. Topics include all the relevant and supporting information you need to master *Microsoft® Project 2007*, and activities allow you to apply this information to practical hands-on examples.

You get to try out each new skill on a specially prepared sample file. This saves you the typing time and allows you to concentrate on the skill at hand. Through the use of sample files, hands-on activities, illustrations that give you feedback at crucial steps, and supporting background information, this book provides you with the foundation and structure to learn *Microsoft® Project 2007* quickly and easily.

As a Review Tool

Any method of instruction is only as effective as the time and effort you are willing to invest in it. In addition, some of the information that you learn in class may not be important to you immediately, but it may become important later on. For this reason, we encourage you to spend some time reviewing the topics and activities after the course. For additional challenge when reviewing activities, try the "What You Do" column before looking at the "How You Do It" column.

As a Reference

The organization and layout of the book make it easy to use as a learning tool and as an after-class reference. You can use this book as a first source for definitions of terms, background information on given topics, and summaries of procedures.

Course Icons

Icon	Description
	A **Caution Note** makes students aware of potential negative consequences of an action, setting, or decision that are not easily known.
	Display Slide provides a prompt to the instructor to display a specific slide. Display Slides are included in the Instructor Guide only.
	An **Instructor Note** is a comment to the instructor regarding delivery, class-room strategy, classroom tools, exceptions, and other special considerations. Instructor Notes are included in the Instructor Guide only.
	Notes Page indicates a page that has been left intentionally blank for students to write on.
	A **Student Note** provide additional information, guidance, or hints about a topic or task.
	A **Version Note** indicates information necessary for a specific version of soft-ware.

Course Objectives

In this course, you will create a project plan containing tasks, organize these tasks in a work breakdown structure containing task relationships, create and assign resources, and finalize the project to implement the project plan.

You will:

- explore the Microsoft Office Project environment and the various views in which you can verify project information.

- create a new project plan.

- manage tasks by organizing them and setting task relationships.

- manage resources in a project plan.

- finalize the project plan.

Course Requirements

Hardware

To use Microsoft Office Project Professional 2007 on each student's machine, you need the following hardware:

- Intel® Pentium® 1.64 MHz or higher processor.
- 512 megabytes (MB) of RAM or more.
- 6 gigabytes (GB) of available hard-disk space or more.
- CD-ROM drive.
- Super VGA or higher resolution monitor.
- Microsoft Mouse, Microsoft IntelliMouse®, or a compatible pointing device.
- A printer.
- A projection system to display the instructor's computer screen.

Software

Software required on each machine includes the following:

- Microsoft® Windows Vista™ Business Edition or Microsoft Windows XP Professional with Service Pack 2.
- Microsoft Office Project Professional 2007.

Class Setup

Install Windows Vista Business Edition

To Install Windows Vista Business Edition:

1. Boot your computer with the DVD containing Business Edition.
2. In the **Install Windows** window, click **Next** to continue the setup.
3. Click the **Install Now** button.
4. In the **Product Key** text box, type the product key of your software and click **Next** to continue.
5. Accept the license agreement and click **Next** to continue.
6. In the **Which Type Of Installation Do You Want** screen, select **Custom (Advanced).**
7. In the **Where do you Want to Install Windows** window, create new partitions with a minimum capacity of 15 GB. Format the partitions to NTFS.
8. Select the C drive partition to install Windows Vista and click **Next** to continue.
9. The computer will automatically restart after a few minutes. Remove the DVD before the system restarts.
10. After finalizing the setup, the computer will restart once again.
11. In the **Type A User Name** text box, enter an account name of **User##**, where ## is a unique number between 1 and 10. Name the Instructor's user account User100.
12. In the **Type A Password** text box, type *p@ssw0rd.*
13. In the **Retype A Password** text box, retype the password to confirm the login details.

14. In the **Type A Password Hint** text box, type *p@ssw0rd* and click **Next** to continue.

15. In the **Type A Computer Name** text box, type a computer name. For the instructor's computer, name the computer Computer100. For student computers, name each one COMPUTER##, where ## is a unique number between 1 and 10–adjust the range accordingly for the number of students in the class.

16. Click **Next** to continue.

17. In the **Help Protect Windows Automatically** screen, click **Use Recommended Settings.**

 To make the data files and activity steps valid please change the system clock date to July 10, 2007.

18. Specify your time and date settings.
   - From the **Time Zone** drop-down list, select your time zone.
   - In the **Date** section, select the date July 10, 2007.
   - If necessary, modify the system time.

19. Click **Next** to continue.

20. On the **Select Your Computer's Current Location** screen, click **Work.**

21. On the **Thank You** screen, click **Start** to start working with Windows Vista.

22. In the **Password** text box, type *p@ssw0rd* and press **Enter.**

Activate Windows Vista

To activate Windows Vista:

1. Choose **Start→Control Panel→System And Maintenance.**

2. Click **System.**

3. In the **Windows Activation** section, click **Activate Windows Now.**

4. If prompted, click **Continue.**

5. In the **Windows Activation** dialog box, click **Activate Windows Online Now.**

6. On the **Activation was Successful** page, click **Close.**

Provide Administrator Rights

To provide Administrator rights:

1. In the **Start** menu, right-click **Computer** and choose **Manage.**

2. In the **User Account Control** dialog box, click **Continue.**

3. In the **Computer Management (Local)** pane, choose **Local Users and Groups→Users.**

4. In the centre pane, right-click **Administrator** and choose **Properties.**

5. In the **Administrator Properties** dialog box, uncheck the **Account is disabled** check box and click **OK.**

6. Choose **Start→Computer.**

7. Right-click **Local Disk (C:)** and choose **Properties.**

8. In the **Local Disk (C:) Properties** dialog box, on the **Security** tab, click **Edit.**

9. Click **Add.**

10. In the **Select Users or Groups** dialog box, click **Advanced** and then click **Find Now.**

11. In the **Search results** section, select **Everyone** and click **OK** two times.

12. In the **Permission for Local Disk (C:)** dialog box, in the **Permission for Everyone** section, in the **Allow** column, check the **Full Control** check box.

13. Click **Apply** and then click **OK** two times.

Install Microsoft Office Project Professional 2007

To install Microsoft® Office Project Professional 2007:

1. Double-click the **setup.exe** file.

2. Enter the product key and click **Continue.**

3. Accept the license agreement and click **Continue.**

4. Click **Install Now.**

5. Once the installation is complete, click **Close.**

Initial Class Setup

1. On the course CD-ROM, run the **084774dd.exe** self-extracting file. This will install a folder named **084774Data** on your C drive. This folder contains all the data files that you will use to complete this course.

2. Navigate to **C:\084774Data** and copy the sub-folders within the **084774Data** folder to the root of the D drive.

3. In the Project window, choose **Tools→Options→Security,** and in the **Legacy Formats** section, select the **Allow loading files with legacy or non default file formats** option and click **OK.**

4. Provide each student with Administrator rights.

5. Verify that file extensions are visible. (In Windows Explorer, choose **Organize→Folder and Search Options** and select the **View** tab. If necessary, uncheck the **Hide Extensions For Known File Types** option and click **OK.**)

6. Install a printer of your choice.

   In addition to the specific setup procedures needed for this class to run properly, you should also check the Element K Press product support website at **http://support.elementkcourseware.com** for more information. Any updates about this course will be posted there.

List of Additional Files

Printed with each activity is a list of files students open to complete that activity. Many activities also require additional files that students do not open, but are needed to support the file(s) students are working with. These supporting files are included with the student data files on the course CD-ROM or data disk. Do not delete these files.

1 | Getting Started with Microsoft Project

Lesson Time: 40 minutes

Lesson Objectives:

In this lesson, you will explore the Microsoft Office Project environment and the various views in which you can verify project information.

You will:

● Explore the Microsoft Project 2007 environment.

● Display an existing project plan in different views.

Introduction

In the planning phases of a project, you would have created many documents, such as a project charter, a team charter, and a statement of work. You are now ready to use your computer to create a project plan, and this requires you to know the features and functioning of the project management tool that will be used. In this lesson, you will explore the features of the Microsoft® Office Project 2007 application.

For a project to be successful, you need to document all information relating to the project in an electronic form, so that data can be analyzed and processed automatically. If you do not know how to use an electronic application for your project management tasks, you will not be able to make the best use of your software tool. This will reduce your chances of executing your projects efficiently or professionally. Using Microsoft Project 2007, you can process any project information with accurate analysis, reduced manual effort, and less error.

TOPIC A
Explore the Microsoft Project 2007 Environment

You have installed Microsoft Project 2007 in your computer. However, you need to launch the application and explore the interface and its functions before you begin working with it. In this topic, you will explore the Microsoft Project 2007 environment.

If you purchased a new device without knowing about its various features and their operation, you will not be able to use the device. Similarly, it is essential to identify the various elements of any new application that is being used for the first time. By exploring the interface of an application, one can be at ease with its features and functions.

Project Management

Project management is the application of knowledge, skills, tools, and techniques to project activities, to further meet the requirements of a project. This is done by integrating the various processes, such as initiation, planning, execution, monitoring, controlling, and closing, involved in management. The project manager is responsible for accomplishing the goals in a project by ensuring that work activities achieve a predefined outcome on time, with quality and within budget.

The Project Management Process

Although each project is unique, there are certain phases that every project should undergo in its life-cycle.

Phase	Activities in the Phase
Initiation	Defining and scoping a project, identifying stake-holders, and building a team.
Planning	Budgeting, scheduling, and planning activities.
Execution	Working the plan, and adapting specifications and plans to the stakeholders' expectations.
Monitoring & Controlling	Monitoring progress; balancing the demands of scope, time, and quality; tracking corrective action; and reporting progress.
Closing	Handing off to end users, closing down operations, and reporting outcomes.

Intiation → Planning → Execution → Monitoring & Controlling → Closing

Figure 1-1: *The various phases of a project's life cycle.*

Microsoft Office Project 2007

Microsoft Office Project 2007 is a project management software that contains a set of tools to help managers plan, schedule, and control their projects. This software is used to create an actual project plan that acts as a repository for all project-related information, including the task list, resources, calendar information, and cost data.

 When you save a **Microsoft Project** plan file, the file gets stored with the **.mpp** extension.

The Microsoft Project Environment

When you launch Microsoft Project 2007, a new blank project file is displayed in the Project application window. In this window, there are various well-organized components that allow users to access the necessary tools and work with this software easily and efficiently.

Interface Component	Description
The Standard toolbar	Provides access to shortcut commands used for opening, closing, and printing a project plan.
The Formatting toolbar	Provides access to frequently used formatting tools, such as font, indent, and field views.
The Project Guide toolbar	Provides detailed instructions and links on the ways to navigate through a project plan.
The Task pane	Appears on the left side of the application window and helps you create a new project from scratch, use an existing project, or create a project from a template.
The entry bar	Appears between the **Project** menu and the **Gantt Chart** view. It allows you to enter and edit information about project tasks.
The active pane indicator	Appears at the left side of any project view, displaying the name of the active view.
The view area	Displays project data. The **Gantt Chart** is the default view.
The table	Shows specific information about tasks, resources, and assignments as a set of fields in a view. The task **Entry** table is displayed in the default view.
The field heading	Appears on the grey area at the top of each column.
The Gantt Chart	Shows task information as a sheet in a project.
The Timescale	Contains the timescale legends for graphically presented tasks or resources.
The divide bar	Separates the table and chart portions of a view. It can be dragged to alter what is visible in the view area.

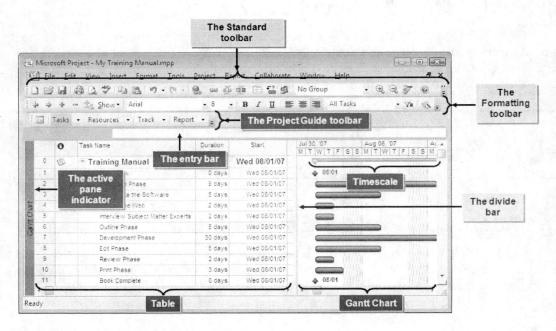

Figure 1-2: *The various components of Microsoft Project 2007.*

ACTIVITY 1-1

Identifying the Screen Elements in Microsoft Project 2007 Environment

Scenario:

As a user who is new to the Microsoft Project environment, you need to test your understanding of the interface elements before creating any new project plans.

---

1. Identify the screen element that helps you create a new project from scratch?

   a) The Standard toolbar

   b) The Task pane

   c) The Gantt Chart

   d) The Project Guide toolbar

2. True or False? During the Monitoring and Controlling phase of project management, the project manager balances the demands of scope, time, and quality; tracks corrective action; and reports progress.

   ___ True

   ___ False

TOPIC B
Display an Existing Project Plan in Different Views

You explored the Microsoft Project 2007 environment. In the Project environment, there are various views in which you can work based on your need. In this topic, you will display an existing project plan in different views.

Let's suppose that you had to describe to your client the budgetary allocation for every phase of a project. It would be effective if you could show the break-up in a pie chart, for different kinds of project information require different kinds of presentation. Microsoft Project helps you to communicate project information effectively through multiple project views.

Microsoft Project Views

Microsoft Project 2007 provides various task, resource, and assignment views. These views display an information subset by using different formats and components.

View Type	Used To
Calendar	Create, edit, show, or review tasks scheduled on specific days, weeks, or months in a calendar.
Gantt Chart	View tasks and associated information in a sheet, and observe tasks and durations over time in a bar graph on a timescale. Use this view to enter and schedule a list of tasks. This view appears by default in Project.
Network Diagram	Enter, edit, and review all tasks and task dependencies in a project. Use this view to create and fine tune your schedule in a flowchart format.
Task Usage	Review, enter, and edit assignments by task. The sheet portion of the view has tasks listed with their assigned resources, and the timesheet portion contains information about the tasks such as work or costs according to the timescale.
Tracking Gantt	Compare the baseline schedule with the actual schedule while implementing a project. In this view, you can view the tasks and task information in a sheet, and a chart showing a baseline and scheduled Gantt bars for each task.
Resource Graph	View resource allocation in a column graph format. When the **Resource Graph** view is used in combination with other views, it is useful for finding over allocation of resources.
Resource Sheet	Enter, edit, and review resource information in a spreadsheet format.
Resource Usage	Review, enter, and edit assignments by resource. The sheet portion of the view contains a list of resources with associated task assignments, and the timesheet portion details the costs or work for the resources on a timescale.

More Views

Besides the commonly used views, Project provides other options for viewing project information with the help of the **More Views** dialog box. Using **More Views** you can observe relationships across variables such as cost, work, and resources in views such as the **Relationship Diagram, Detail Gantt, Descriptive Network Diagram,** and **Resource Allocation.**

View Formats

Views in Microsoft Project use several display formats to present different kinds of information graphically.

View Format	Description
Sheet	Resembles a spreadsheet or a table of information.
Graph	Provides an illustration of a project's schedule or progress.
Diagram	Displays the tasks in a flowchart format. This format can be helpful in fine tuning your schedule.
Usage	Lists task or resource data on the left side and shows time-phased data across rows and columns on the right side.
Form	Presents and parallelly displays detailed information about a task or resource in a structured format.

Timescale

A timescale is the range of period within which work has elapsed. In Microsoft Project, timescale is the time period indicator that appears at the top of the time-phased portion of various project views. In a project, the timescale helps you identify and define the period during which a task is to be completed or a resource is available.

 In Microsoft Project, timescale appears as an indicator in various project views, such as the **Gantt Chart, Resource Graph, Task Usage,** and **Resource Usage.**

How to Display an Existing Project Plan in Different Views

Procedure Reference: Open an Existing Project Plan

To open an existing project plan:

1. Launch the Microsoft Office Project 2007 application.

    ● Choose **Start→All Programs→Microsoft Office→Microsoft Office Project 2007.**

    ● Or, on the desktop, double-click the **Microsoft Office Project 2007** icon.

2. Display the **Open** dialog box.

    ● From the menu, choose **File→Open.**

    ● On the **Standard** toolbar, click the **Open** button.

    ● Or, on the keyboard, press **Ctrl+O.**

3. Find the folder that contains the project plan.

    ● In the **Open** dialog box, in the Navigation pane, click **Folders** to display the **Folders** list.

    ● If necessary, click and drag **Folders** to the top of the Navigation pane.

    ● Or, in the **Type to search the current view** text box, type the name of the folder.

4. In the Navigation pane, in the **Folders** list, click to open the desired folder that contains the project plan.

5. Open the project plan with the .mpp extension.

    ● In the file list area, select the file, and click **Open.**

    ● Or, in the file list area, double-click the file.

Procedure Reference: Display an Existing Plan in Different Project Views

To display an existing project in different views:

1. Open the project file you want to view.

2. If necessary, display the **View Bar.**

    ● From the menu, choose **View→View Bar.**

    ● Or, right-click the active pane indicator and choose **View Bar.**

3. Display the project plan in the desired view.

    ● From the **View** menu, choose the desired view option.

    ● Right-click the active pane indicator and choose the desired view option.

    ● Or, on the **View Bar,** click the desired view icon.

4. If necessary, display the project plan using a view in the **More Views** dialog box.

    a. Display the **More Views** dialog box.

    ● From the menu, choose **View→More Views.**

    ● Right-click the active pane indicator, and choose **More Views.**

    ● Or, on the **View Bar,** click **More Views.**

    b. Display the desired view.

    ● In the **Views** list box, double-click the desired view.

    ● Or, select the view and click **Apply.**

ACTIVITY 1-2

Displaying a Project File in Different Views

Data Files:

CSS Training Manual.mpp

Scenario:

The project management team uses Microsoft Project 2007 to create, monitor, and implement the project plans. You have newly joined the team as a project lead. You need to know the various formats available for viewing the information. You have been asked to look at the CSS Training Manual.mpp file and then view information related to tasks and resources.

What You Do	How You Do It
1. Launch Microsoft Office Project 2007.	a. On the Windows task bar, click the **Start** button to display the **Start** menu.
	b. In the **Start** menu, position the mouse pointer over **All Programs** to display all the programs.
	c. In the **All Programs** submenu, choose **Microsoft Office** to view a list of the **Microsoft Office** applications.
	d. Choose **Microsoft Office Project 2007** to launch the application.
	e. In the **Welcome to the 2007 Microsoft Office system** dialog box, click **Next**.
	f. Select **I don't want to use Microsoft Update** option to decline the usage of **Microsoft Update** and click **Finish.**

2. Open the **CSS Training Manual.mpp** file in its default view.

   a. From the menu, choose **File→Open.**

   b. In the **Open** dialog box, in the Navigation pane, click **Folders** to display the **Folders** list.

   c. Select and drag the **Folders** tab to the top of the Navigation pane.

   d. Navigate to the **C:\084774Data\Getting Started** folder.

   e. In the file list area, select **CSS Training Manual.mpp** and click **Open.**

   f. Notice that the file opens in the **Gantt Chart** view by default, listing information about the tasks in the project.

3. **What is the default view in Project? What table is applied to the default view?**

4. Display the file in different views.

   a. Choose **View→Resource Sheet** to display information on resources in a sheet, where you can enter and edit resource information.

   b. Choose **View→Network Diagram** to view project tasks and task dependencies.

   c. Choose **View→Task Usage** to display a task sheet, where you can review, enter, and edit assignments by task.

   d. Choose **File→Save** to save the file.

   e. Choose **File→Close** to close the file.

   f. Choose **File→Close** to close the **Project1** file.

Lesson 1 Follow-up

In this lesson, you explored the features and functions of the Microsoft Office Project environment. You also viewed the project data in various views. Acquainting yourself with the components of the Project interface helps you efficiently complete your projects.

1. **How can Microsoft Project enhance your approach to planning in project management?**

2. **While exploring the Microsoft Project environment, what are the components you found to be useful for your work?**

Primavera
Pert

Task → Activity

Change Dependencies

EMOP || PERT

$$E = [O + P + (4 * M)] / 6$$

  Opt   Pess   Middle

DURATION — 1 DAY	2
WORK — 8 HRS	16
ASSIGNMENT — 100%	
(UNITS)	

MILESTONE : & DURATION; CRITICAL POINT IN TIME
           AS AN ACCOMPLISHMENT

2 | Creating a Project Plan

Lesson Time: 1 hour(s), 30 minutes

Lesson Objectives:

In this lesson, you will create a new project plan.

You will:

- Create a project plan.
- Assign a project calendar.
- Add tasks to the project plan.
- Enter the duration estimates for tasks.
- Add resources into the project plan.

Introduction

You explored the features, functions, and the various views of the Project environment. Now, you need to use Project to create an electronic project plan that will contain the complete project-related information, which will be used to work out and follow the project schedule. In this lesson, you will create a project plan, which will include the project start date, project calendar, project tasks and their durations, and the resources involved.

For your project to be successful, it is imperative that you accurately define it within Microsoft Project. This will be easy if you have done all the preliminary work of creating a complete and accurate project plan. Neglecting to enter relevant project information, including your company's working schedule, or tasks into your project plan can impact whether or not your project will finish on time, within budget, and within scope.

TOPIC A
Create a New Project Plan

You completed the initiation and planning phases of a project. You are ready to use Microsoft Project as a tool to create a project plan. In this topic, you will create and save a project plan that contains general project information such as the project start date, the project title, and the project manager's name.

Keeping track of project tasks, resources, costs, and schedules can be an overwhelming task. By entering your approved project plan information into Microsoft Project, you can automate much of your project management efforts by accessing one repository for all your project-related components, as well as stay organized and save time. Creating the actual project plan is the first step in this process.

The Project Guide

The **Project Guide,** which is displayed by default, is a tool that helps you navigate through the project management process by displaying detailed instructions and controls.

Element	Description
The Project Guide toolbar	Provides access to assistance in each of the goal areas—tasks, resources, track, and report.
The Side pane	Contains a list of tasks for each activity in each goal area along with helpful instructions, wizards, and links. The steps that appear in the side pane of the **Project Guide** do not have to be performed in a specified order.
The View area	Appears to the right of the side pane and changes depending on the task you execute in the side pane.

Tables

Tables control the kind of information you want to present about tasks, resources, and assignments in a sheet view. By choosing a table from the **View** menu, you can display various tables and control the columns or fields that appear in the table. Tables display your project data in a horizontal row format, with each task and its related information appearing in a single row.

 To apply a table to a view, from the menu, choose **View→Table: Entry** and then select the desired table from the list.

A Cell

The intersection of a column and a row is called a cell. You can use the arrow keys to move from cell to cell in a table, or press **Tab** to move one column to the right. You can also press **Home** to move to the **Indicators** column of the selected row.

Fields

A *field* is a location in a sheet, form, or chart that contains a specific kind of information about a task, a resource, or an assignment. It is either part of a table, a form view, or a timephased area of the usage views. For example, the task **Entry** table, displayed in the **Gantt Chart** view, displays the **Task Name, Duration, Start, Finish, Predecessors,** and **Resource Names** fields for each task within your project. If you need to display specific values or information that are unique to your project, you can create custom fields. To set a custom field, choose **Tools→Customize→Fields.**

The Project Information Dialog Box

Project scheduling is a key factor in the decision-making process of a project. Using the **Project Information** dialog box, you can schedule your organization's projects and tasks with available resources. If you enter a **Start date** for the project, by default, Project schedules tasks to begin on the project's start date, and calculates the project's **Finish date** based on the last task to finish. You can also specify the type of calendar you want to set as your project calendar through the **Calendar** option.

Project Scheduling from a Project End Date

Although most projects will be scheduled from a known start date, there may be times when you are forced to schedule from a finish date. An example of when you will schedule a project from a finish date could be perhaps when you receive work from an outside source and have not yet been told when it is to start. However, you have been told when it must finish. If you must schedule from a finish date, choose **Project→Project Information.** In the **Project Information** dialog box, enter the project finish date in the **Finish date** text box. When scheduling from a project finish date, keep in mind that Project will handle some actions very differently.

The Timescale Dialog Box

The **Timescale** dialog box is used to specify and format the view options for the three tiers or units in a timescale.

Tab	Description
Top Tier	Specifies the default time unit as months for the top timescale tier. This tab appears when you choose to show all three available tiers.
Middle Tier	Specifies the default time unit as weeks for the middle timescale tier. This tab appears when you choose to show at least two of the three available tiers.
Bottom Tier	Specifies the default time unit as days for the bottom timescale tier. This tab appears when you choose to show any of the three available tiers.

The File Properties Dialog Box

The **File Properties** dialog box provides various tabs for entering the general information about a project plan.

Tab	Description
General	Displays various information, such as file name, type, size, location of the file and its attributes, about the project.
Summary	Allows you to enter the project information such as the manager's name, the name of the company, the subject, and title of the project.
Statistics	Indicates the access properties, such as the time of creation and modification, of the file.
Contents	Specifies the content, such as the start and finish dates, duration of the project, total work hours, cost of the project, and the percentage of work completed.
Custom	Displays project information that can be customized in terms of the person or the department that has verified the document, and other file properties such as the status of completion of work.

How to Create a New Project Plan

Procedure Reference: Create a New Project Plan Using the Project Guide Toolbar

To create a new project plan using the **Project Guide** toolbar:

1. Choose **File→New** to display the **New Project** task pane.
2. Activate the **Project Guide** toolbar.
   - From the menu, choose **View→Turn On Project Guide.**
   - Or, display the **Project Guide** toolbar using the **Options** dialog box.
     a. Choose **Tools→Options.**
     b. In the **Options** dialog box, on the **Interface** tab, in the **Project Guide settings** section, check the **Display Project Guide** check box.
     c. In the **Options** dialog box, click **OK.**
3. Display a blank new project plan.
   - In the **New Project** task pane, in the **New** section, click **Blank Project.**
   - Or, on the **Standard** toolbar, click the **New** button.
4. If necessary, on the **Project Guide** toolbar, click **Tasks** to display the **Tasks** side pane.
5. In the **Tasks** side pane, click the **Define the project** link to launch the **Define the project** side pane for defining a project.

6.   Enter the start date of your project.

- In the **Define the Project** side pane, in the **Enter the estimated date your project will begin** text box, enter the desired date.

- Or, in the **Define the Project** side pane, click the **Enter the estimated date your project will begin** drop-down arrow to display a calendar. And in the calendar, navigate to the desired project start date and select the date.

7.   At the bottom of the **Define the Project** side pane, click the **Continue to Step 2** link.

8.   In the **Define the Project** side pane, respond to the **Collaborate on your project** question.

- Select the **Yes** option to use a web server to update project information.

- Select the **No** option to decline the use of a web server to update project information.

9.   At the bottom of the **Define the Project** side pane, click the **Continue to Step 3** link.

10. At the bottom of the **Define the Project** side pane, click the **Save and Finish** link to complete the project definition.

11. Save the file.

    a.   Display the **Save As** dialog box.

- Choose **File→Save As.**

- On the **Standard** toolbar, click **Save.**

- Or, on the keyboard, press **Ctrl+S.**

    b.   In the **File name** text box, type the desired name for the file.

    c.   Click **Save.**

Hiding the Project Guide Toolbar

To prevent the **Project Guide** toolbar from being displayed, choose **Tools→Options,** select the **Interface** tab, and under the **Project Guide settings** section, uncheck the **Display Project Guide** check box.

Create a New Project Using Project Information Dialog Box

Apart from using the **Project Guide** toolbar to create a new file, you can use the **Project Information** dialog box to create a new project. From the menu, choose **Project→Project Information** and enter the project start date in the **Start Date** text box, and then click **OK.** Then, save the file with a unique file name to a preferred location.

Procedure Reference: Schedule a Project from a Project Start Date

To schedule a project from a project start date:

1.   Open an existing project plan.

2.   From the menu, choose **Project→Project Information** to display the **Project Information** dialog box.

3.   From the **Schedule from** drop-down list, select **Project Start Date** to schedule a project from the start date.

4.   Enter the start date of the project.

- In the **Project Information** dialog box, in the **Start date** text box, type the desired start date of the project.

- Or, in the **Project Information** dialog box, click the **Start date** drop-down arrow, navigate to the desired start date, and select it.

5.   In the **Project Information** dialog box, click **OK** and save the file.

Procedure Reference: Define the File Properties of a Project

To define the file properties of a project:

1.   Open an existing project plan.
2.   From the menu, choose **File→Properties** to display the project's **Properties** dialog box.
3.   On the **Summary** tab, enter the necessary details relevant to the project.
4.   Click **OK** to close the **Properties** dialog box.

Procedure Reference: Change the Timescale of a Project

To change the timescale of a project:

1.   Open an existing project plan.
2.   From the menu, choose **Format→Timescale** to display the **Timescale** dialog box.
3.   Select the desired tab of the tier you want to modify.
4.   In the **Timescale options** section, from the **Show** drop-down list, select the desired change to display the chosen tier level.
5.   If necessary, select any other tier tab and make the desired changes.
6.   Click **OK** to apply the changes made in the **Timescale** dialog box and save the file.

ACTIVITY 2-1

Creating a New Project Plan Using the Project Guide Toolbar

Before You Begin:

The Microsoft Project application is open.

Scenario:

As an employee of Our Global Company, you have been newly appointed as a project manager for the development of a training manual. The initiation and planning phases of the project are complete. Now, you want to plan your project and enter information using Microsoft Project as a tool. You also know that the project starts on August 1, 2007.

What You Do	How You Do It
1. Open a blank project plan.	a. From the menu, choose **File→New** to display the **New Project** side pane.
	b. In the **New Project** side pane, in the **New** section, click **Blank Project.**

2. Define the project using the **Project Guide** toolbar.

   a. From the menu, choose **View→Turn On Project Guide** to display the **Project Guide** toolbar.

   b. In the **Tasks** side pane, click the **Define the project** link.

   c. In the **Define the Project** side pane, click the **Enter the estimated date your project will begin** drop-down arrow to display the calendar.

   d. In the calendar, click the right arrow twice to navigate to the month of August.

   e. In the **August, 2007** calendar, select **1** as the date.

   f. At the bottom of the **Define the Project** side pane, click the **Continue to Step 2** link.

   g. In the **Collaborate on your project** section, verify that the **No** option is selected.

   h. At the bottom of the **Define the Project** side pane, click the **Continue to Step 3** link.

   i. At the bottom of the **Define the Project** side pane, click the **Save and Finish** link.

3. Save the project file as *My Training Manual.mpp*

   a. From the menu, choose **File→Save As.**

   b. In the **Save As** dialog box, navigate to the **C:\084774Data\Creating a Project Plan** folder.

   c. In the **File name** text box, click and type *My Training Manual.mpp*

   d. Click **Save.**

4. Enter the file properties for the project plan.

a. From the menu, choose **File→Properties** to display the **My Training Manual.mpp Properties** dialog box.

b. On the **Summary** tab, in the **Subject** text box, click and type *Training Manual*

c. In the **Manager** text box, type your name.

d. In the **Company** text box, click and type *Our Global Company*

e. In the **Comments** text box, click and type *Our goal is to market quality products.*

f. Click **OK.**

g. On the **Standard** toolbar, click the **Save** button.

TOPIC B
Assign a Project Calendar

You created and saved a new project plan. For Project to correctly calculate a schedule for the created project, the company's working times should be given as an input. In this topic, you will create a project calendar that includes your company's working and non-working times, and then assign that calendar to your project plan.

One of the benefits of using Project is that it will create a schedule for all tasks in your project plan. To ensure that project tasks do not get scheduled to be executed at midnight or on company holidays, you will need to specify and assign a project calendar that includes your company's working and non-working times.

Base Calendars in Microsoft Project 2007

A project must base its schedule on some measure of time. Microsoft Project uses *base calendars* to create a schedule for a project. A base calendar is used as a template for scheduling the standard working time, which includes work hours for each day and work days for each week. The base calendar also includes non-working times and any exceptions such as holidays.

> You can also create your own base calendars, which is useful if you have alternative schedules for multiple resources. For example, you might have resources working part-time, 12–hour shifts, or on weekends.

Project has three default base calendars—**Standard, 24 Hours,** and **Night Shift.**

Base Calendar	Description
Standard	Reflects a traditional work schedule of Monday through Friday, 8:00 A.M. to 5:00 P.M. with a 1-hour break. This is the default base calendar for project, resource, and task calendars.
24 Hours	Reflects a schedule with no non-working time for projects that are worked on around the clock. This calendar can be used to schedule resources and tasks for different shifts round the clock, or to schedule equipment resources continuously.
Night Shift	Reflects a shift schedule of Monday night through Saturday morning, 11:00 P.M. to 8:00 A.M. with a 1-hour break.

Calendar Types

Project provides various types of calendars to define the working hours or days, and non-working time for an entire project, or even for individual resources and tasks.

Calendar Type	Description
Project calendar	The base calendar that specifies the default working and non-working times for a project. The **Standard** base calendar is the default project calendar.
Resource calendar	A calendar created to specify working and non-working times for an individual resource when exceptions from the base calendar exist. The **Standard** base calendar is the default resource calendar.
Task calendar	A calendar applied to an individual task created to control the scheduling of a task when exceptions from the base calendar exist. By default, all tasks are scheduled according to the project calendar.

The Change Working Time Dialog Box

The options in the **Change Working Time** dialog box allow you to create, review, and modify the base and project calendars for a project, resource, or task.

Option	Description
For calendar	Provides the available list of base and project calendars for your project.
Legend	Displays an index of color boxes with a description for each colored box that includes the working, non-working times, and exception days or hours in your base calendar.
Click on a day to see its working times	Displays a preview of your project calendar with its working times, or any exceptions on a particular date.
Exceptions	Allows you to set occasional variances to normal working hours, such as holidays and personal time off.
Work Weeks	Allows you to set up the normal week for the selected calendar.
Details	Allows you to specify changes to days of the week in the **Details** dialog box.
Create New Calendar	Allows you to create a new base calendar for your project using the **Create New Base Calendar** dialog box.

How to Assign a Project Calendar

Procedure Reference: Create a Project Calendar with General Working Hours

To create a project calendar with general working hours:

1. Open the desired project plan and if necessary, display the **Project Guide** toolbar.

2. On the **Project Guide** toolbar, click **Tasks.**

3. In the **Tasks** side pane, click the **Define general working times** link to display the **Preview Working Time** calendar on the right side.

4. In the **Project Working Times** side pane, from the **Select a calendar template** drop-down list, select the desired base calendar, and on the Step 1 of 5 section, click the **Continue to Step 2** link.

5. If necessary, in the **Define the work week** section, check the check boxes from Monday through Friday, and select the **I'll use the hours shown in the preview on the right** option.

6. At the bottom of the **Project Working Times** side pane, in the **Step 2 of 5** section, click the **Continue to Step 3** link.

7. If necessary, in the **Set Holidays and Days Off** section, click the **Change Working Time** link to launch the **Change Working Time** dialog box and change the working hours.

8. At the bottom of the **Project Working Times** side pane, in the **Step 3 of 5** section, click the **Continue to Step 4** link.

9. If necessary, in the **Define time units** section, in the **Hours per day, Hours per week,** and **Days per month** text boxes, enter the desired time respectively. In the **Step 4 of 5** section, click the **Continue to Step 5** link.

10. In the **Project Working Times** side pane, in the **Step 5 of 5** section, click the **Save and Finish** link to set the project calendar.

Procedure Reference: Create a Project Calendar with the Desired Working Hours

To create a project calendar with the desired working hours:

1. From the menu, choose **Tools→Change Working Time** to display the **Change Working Time** dialog box.

2. Click **Create New Calendar** and in the **Create New Calendar** dialog box, specify the settings for the new calendar.

   - In the **Name** text box, type the name of the new calendar, and select the **Create new base calendar** option and click **OK** to return to the **Change Working Time** dialog box.

   - If necessary, select the **Make a copy of calendar** option and from the **Make a copy of calendar** drop-down list, select the desired calendar for making a copy. Click **OK.**

3. If necessary, in the **Change Working Time** dialog box, select the **Work Weeks** tab, and select the row in the table that indicates the default schedule. Click the **Details** button to display the **Details** dialog box and specify the new working times.

    ● In the **Set working time for this work week** section, in the **Select day(s)** list box, select the desired day of the week, and select the **Use Project default times for these days** option to select the default work week. Click **OK** to return to the **Change Working Time** dialog box.

    ● In the **Select day(s)** list box, press **Ctrl** to select multiple days or press **Shift** to select consecutive days, and select the **Set days to non-working time** option to make the selected days as non-working days.

    ● Select the day(s), and select the **Set day(s) to these specific working times** option to display the working times table. Then, specify the working times in the working times table and click **OK.**

4. Set changes to the working times of the calendar as exceptions.

    ● Select the **Exceptions** tab and in the **Name** column, select the available row and type the name of the exception.

    ● Type the **Start** and **Finish** date or select the dates from the drop-down calendars for the exception. Click **OK** to save the changes made in the **Change Working Time** dialog box.

    ● If necessary, with the exception row still selected, use the **Details** button to specify non default working times or hours for the exception dates.

Procedure Reference: Assign a Calendar to a Project

To assign a calendar to a project:

1. Open the desired project plan and from the menu, choose **Project→Project Information.**

2. In the **Project Information** dialog box, from the **Calendar** drop-down list, select the desired calendar.

3. Click **OK.**

ACTIVITY 2-2

Assigning a Calendar to a Project

Data Files:

My Training Manual.mpp

Before You Begin:

The My Training Manual.mpp file is open.

Scenario:

The Human Resources department has issued a list of company holidays and time off for the year 2007. As the project manager for the training manual project, you want to ensure that Project considers these company holidays when scheduling your project. Here's the company's holiday list:

● September 3, 2007 (Labor Day)

● November 22 and 23, 2007 (On account of Thanksgiving)

● December 24 to 28, 2007 (Christmas)

● December 21, 2007 (Holiday Luncheon—All employees to work half a day, from 8:00 A.M.–12:00 P.M.)

What You Do	How You Do It

1. **Does the Project Guide toolbar offer any options for working with calendars?**

 Although the **Project Guide** toolbar does offer a link for defining general working times, you will use the menu to perform this activity.

2. Create a new calendar named *Our Global Company.*

   a. In the **Tasks** side pane, click the **Close** button.

   b. From the menu, choose **Tools→Change Working Time** to display the **Change Working Time** dialog box.

   c. Click **Create New Calendar** to display the **Create New Base Calendar** dialog box.

   d. In the **Name** text box, type *Our Global Company*

   e. In the **Make a copy of calendar** drop-down list, verify that the **Standard** base calendar is selected and click **OK.**

3. **What is the default project calendar?**

4. **What are the defaults for the work week and for the work-day hours?**

5. Specify the company holidays as non-working days.

    a. On the **Exceptions** tab, select the first row, in the **Name** column, click and type *Labor Day* and press **Enter.**

    b. In the first row, in the **Start** column, click, type *09/03/2007* and press **Enter.**

    c. Observe that in the first row, in the **Finish** column, the date **09/03/2007** is auto-populated.

    d. In the **Click on a day to see its working times** calendar preview, scroll down to **November 2007.**

    e. In the calendar preview, select **22,** hold down **Shift,** and select **23.**

    f. On the **Exceptions** tab, select the second row, in the **Name** column, click and type *On account of Thanksgiving* and press **Enter.**

    g. In the **Click on a day to see its working times** calendar preview, scroll down to **December 2007.**

    h. In the calendar preview, select **24,** hold down **Shift,** and select **28.**

    i. On the **Exceptions** tab, select the third row, in the **Name** column, click and type *Christmas* and press **Enter.**

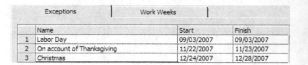

	Name	Start	Finish
1	Labor Day	09/03/2007	09/03/2007
2	On account of Thanksgiving	11/22/2007	11/23/2007
3	Christmas	12/24/2007	12/28/2007

6. **What indication do you receive that these dates have been marked as non-working days?**

7. Specify the non default work days.

    a. In the calendar preview, in the month of **December 2007**, select **21.**

    b. Select the **Work Weeks** tab and in the **Name** column, select the row after the **[Default]** working time row.

    c. In the **Name** column, type **Luncheon** and press **Enter.**

    d. In the **Name** column, select **Luncheon** and click **Details.**

    e. In the **Details for 'Luncheon'** dialog box, in the **Select day(s)** list box, select **Friday.**

    f. Select the **Set day(s) to these specific working times** option to change the day to a half a day working day.

    g. In the second row, in the **From** column, select **1:00 PM** and press **Delete** to delete the afternoon working hours from 1 PM to 5 PM.

    h. Click **OK** to close the **Details for 'Luncheon'** dialog box.

    i. In the **Change Working Time** dialog box, click **OK** to save the changes for the non-working days in the project calendar.

8. Assign the **Our Global Company** calendar to the training manual project.

    a. From the menu, choose **Project→Project Information** to display the **Project Information for 'My Training Manual.mpp'** dialog box.

    b. From the **Calendar** drop-down list, select **Our Global Company.**

    c. Click **OK.**

    d. Save the file.

TOPIC C
Add Tasks to the Project Plan

You created a project plan and assigned a project calendar to it. You now need to specify the tasks that are required to complete your project. In this topic, you will add tasks into the project plan.

For Project to calculate a schedule, you must enter tasks. Without tasks, there would not be a project plan, as tasks are the building blocks for the rest of the plan. It is through this plan that you are able to calculate the project schedule, assign project resources, and determine project costs.

Tasks

Definition:

A *task* is an individual work item that defines a piece of work required to complete a project. All tasks contain a **Task Name.** They require an estimated amount of time for execution, known as the duration, which is indicated by the start and finish time. When you enter a task into the project plan, Project assigns **1 day?,** with a question mark indicating an estimate as the default duration value. Later, Project will calculate the start and finish dates for the tasks based on the project's start and finish dates. To avoid confusion, all tasks should have unique task names.

 If you have a task list in another file format, such as **Microsoft Excel,** you can import these tasks lists using the **Open** dialog box.

Example:

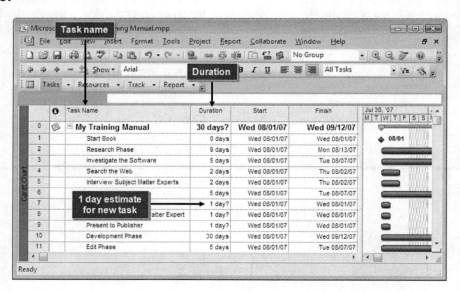

Task Categories

Various categories of tasks are used to identify a task's hierarchical position.

Task Category	Description
Project summary task	Indicates the highest level of work in a project and represents the project goal or project objective. All other project tasks are represented as subtasks beneath the project summary task.
Summary task	Contains the broad concepts of projects, and is represented in the **Gantt Chart** by black bars with black triangular end points. The start date of a summary task is determined by the earliest start date of any of its subtasks.
Subtask	Contains the detailed steps necessary to complete the summary tasks, and is represented in the **Gantt Chart** as blue bars. The schedule and cost information from subtasks are accumulated at the summary task level.

How to Add Tasks in the Project Plan

Procedure Reference: Add Tasks in the Project Plan

To add tasks in the project plan:

1. If necessary, open the project plan in the **Gantt Chart** view.
2. Enter the summary tasks.

    a. In the **Entry** table, in the desired row, in the **Task Name** field, type a task name.

    b. Press **Enter** so that the task name is entered into the **Entry** table and the active cell moves down to the next row.

 Although it makes sense to enter the task in the order that they will occur, it is easy to insert and relocate a task within the **Entry** table.

    c. Repeat steps a and b until all the tasks have been entered in the project plan.

 If you inadvertently double-click a task name in the **Entry** table, the **Task Information** dialog box is displayed. Click **OK** to close it.

3. Enter the subtasks.

    a. In the **Entry** table, select the task for which you want to create subtasks.

    b. Insert a new row in the **Entry** table.

    • From the menu, choose **Insert→New Task.**

- Or, press **Insert.**

c. Enter the subtask name in the Task Name field.

d. Repeat steps b and c until all the subtasks for the summary task have been entered.

The Change Highlighting Feature

You will be able to notice that the changes in the task **Entry** table for the **Duration, Start,** and **Finish** columns for the newly entered task are highlighted in blue. Project highlights corresponding changes made to any information in the project plan, with the help of the **Change Highlighting** feature. To activate the **Change Highlighting** feature, from the menu, choose **View→Show Change Highlighting.**

Task Editing Options

It is possible that the tasks in your project plan will change. The steps to edit tasks are displayed in the following table.

Edit Result	*Procedure*
Edit text in a cell	1. Select the task name.
	2. Place the insertion point on the entry bar, and then edit one or more characters using the arrow keys, **Backspace,** and **Delete.**
	3. Press **Enter** or click the green check mark.
Move a task	1. Select the entire task by clicking the ID number for the task.
	2. Relocate the task.
	• From the menu, choose **Edit→Cut Task.**
	• Right-click the ID number and choose **Cut Task.**
	• Or, press **Ctrl+X.**
	3. Click in the row where you want the task to appear.
	4. Paste the task in the new location.
	• From the menu, choose **Edit→Paste.**
	• Right-click the ID number and choose **Paste.**
	• Or, press **Ctrl+V.**

Edit Result	**Procedure**
Copy a task	1. Select the entire task by clicking the ID number for the task.
	2. Copy the task.
	• From the menu, choose **Edit→Copy Task.**
	• Right-click the ID number and choose **Copy Task.**
	• Or, press **Ctrl+C.**
	3. Click in the row where you want the task to appear.
	4. From the menu, choose **Edit→Paste.**
Adjust column width	1. Place the mouse pointer over the column head divider.
	2. Double-click.
Adjust row height	1. Place the mouse pointer over the row divider.
	2. Drag up or down.
Insert a task	1. Select the task below the row where you want the new task inserted.
	2. Press **Insert.**
Delete a task	1. Select the entire task by clicking on the ID number for the task.
	2. Press **Delete.**
Undo a mistake	• From the menu, choose **Edit→Undo.**
	• On the **Standard** toolbar, click the **Undo** button.
	• Or, press **Ctrl+Z.**

Procedure Reference: Display a Project Summary Task

To display a project summary task:

1. Display the **View** tab of the **Options** dialog box.

2. On the **View** tab, in the **Outline options for (project)** section, check the **Show project summary task** check box.

3. If necessary, deselect the other check boxes except the **Show summary task** check box to display the summary task. Click **OK.** In the **Task Name** column, a new **Project summary task** appears with the task name in bold, and the task ID number as 0.

4. If necessary, select the **Project summary task** name and type the desired text.

ACTIVITY 2-3

Entering Tasks into the Project Plan

Data Files:

My Training Manual.mpp

Before You Begin:

The My Training Manual.mpp file is open.

Scenario:

During a brainstorming session held in the planning phase of the project, the project team identified that the project's goal is to bring out a training manual. Also, the project team brought out a list of probable phases of the project and also the jobs in one of the phases. You need to include the same in your project.

What You Do	How You Do It
1. Enter the summary tasks.	a. In the **Entry** table, in the first row, in the **Task Name** column, type *Start Book*
	b. Press **Enter** so that the task name is entered into the **Entry** table and the active cell moves down to the next row.
	c. Observe that the values in the **Duration, Start,** and **Finish** columns of the **Start Book** task in the **Entry** table are highlighted in blue.
	d. Enter the other task names for the project: *Research Phase, Outline Phase, Development Phase, Test Phase, Review Phase, Print Phase,* and *Book Complete.*

2. **What are the screen changes that have occurred as a result of entering the Start Book task?**

3. Edit Task 5 to read *Edit Phase.*

    a. In the **Entry** table, select Task 5, **Test Phase.**

    b. In the entry bar, double-click the word **Test,** type *Edit* to replace the selected word, and press **Enter.**

4. Display all the fields in the task **Entry** table.

    a. Position the mouse pointer on the divide bar between the task **Entry** table and the **Gantt Chart.** Notice that the mouse pointer changes to a horizontal double-headed arrow.

    b. Drag the mouse approximately 3 inches to the right till the **Resource Names** column is visible in the **Entry** table.

5. Type the subtasks for Task 2, the **Research Phase** summary task.

    a. In the **Entry** table, select the **Outline Phase** task and from the menu, choose **Insert→New Task.**

    b. In the third row, in the **Task Name** field, type *Interview Subject Matter Experts* and press **Enter.**

    c. Position the mouse pointer on the column divider between the **Task Name** and **Duration** columns and when the mouse pointer changes to a horizontal double-headed arrow, double-click to increase the width of the column.

    d. Enter the other subtasks: *Investigate the Software* and *Search the Web.*

6. Relocate Task 3, **Interview Subject Matter Experts,** as Task 5.

    a. Click the ID number for Task 3, **Interview Subject Matter Experts,** to select the entire task.

 To move the entire task, be certain to select the ID number.

b. Choose **Edit→Cut Task.**

c. Click the ID number for Task 5 and choose **Edit→Paste.**

d. Click Task 6 to view the relocated task clearly.

---

7. Display the project summary task.

a. From the menu, choose **Tools→Options** to display the **Options** dialog box.

b. On the **View** tab, in the **Outline options for 'My Training Manual.mpp'** section, check the **Show project summary task** check box and click **OK** to display the project summary task.

c. Observe that in the **Task Name** column, the project summary task with the name **My Training Manual** task appears in bold and the task ID number appears as **0.**

d. Save the file.

TOPIC D
Enter the Task Duration Estimates

You created an activity plan that contains a list of tasks. Without knowing the durations of the tasks, it would be difficult to plan your project. In this topic, you will enter the task duration estimates.

For Project to accurately schedule the tasks in your project plan, you must enter estimated durations for each task. Without durations, your project plan would be nothing more than a to-do list.

Duration

Definition:

Duration is the time interval between the start and end time of a task. Project assigns an estimate of a 1-day duration to each new task in the project plan. Day is the default parameter, and Project calculates 1 day as 8 hours, 1 week as 40 hours, and 1 month as 20 working days. There are other parameters such as minutes and hours to estimate the duration of the tasks. The duration settings can be altered using the **Calendar** tab of the **Options** dialog box.

 The best practice is to enter duration estimates for tasks, thereby allowing Project to schedule the task start and finish dates. Do not enter task start and finish dates.

Example:

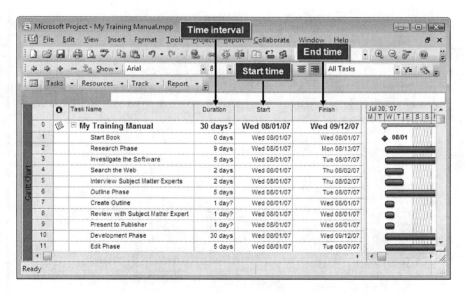

Duration Codes

The duration codes of the other parameters that can be used in a project are displayed in the following table.

Duration	Displayed As
Minutes	m, min, minute.
Hours	h, hr, hour.
Days	d, dy, day.
Weeks	w, wk, week.
Elapsed Duration	emin, ehr, eday, ewk. Use elapsed duration when 24 hours by 7 days of continuous effort is needed. Usually used for unattended tasks such as allowing paint to dry or concrete to set.

The Duration Formula

When estimating the duration of tasks, it is helpful to seek the advice of people involved in the tasks. You can also create an estimated duration by using the $E = [O + P + (4 * M)]/6$ formula, where:

- E = estimated duration.
- M = the most probable time.
- O = the most optimistic time (5% probability).
- P = the most pessimistic time (5% probability).

For example, if the optimistic duration is 2 weeks(w), the pessimistic duration is 10 weeks, and the most likely duration is 3 weeks, then the estimated duration is $[2w + 10w + (4*3w)]/6 = 4$ weeks.

Work

Definition:

Work is the amount of person-hours needed to complete each resource's assignment. The total work for a task is the sum of the work of all its assignments. The formula for calculating work is Work = Duration * Units. The total amount of time spent by the resource for its assigned tasks varies based on the nature of the task and the efficiency of the resource.

Example:

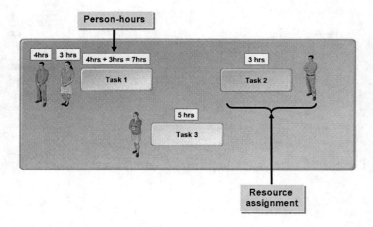

Units

Definition:

A **unit** is the representation of the percentage of a resource's time assigned to a task. The default percentage is 100. However, if a resource would work only half-time on a task, you can set that resource's assignment units to 50 percent.

Example:

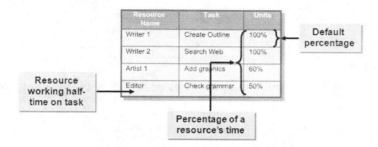

Milestone

Definition:

A **milestone** is a task that acts as a reference point, which marks a major event in a project and is used to monitor the project's progress. As a general rule, you use milestones to mark the beginning and end of your project, the end of a major phase, or for a task for which the duration is unknown or out of your control. In the **Gantt Chart,** milestones are displayed with the symbol of a black diamond. Any task with zero duration is automatically displayed as a milestone. You can also mark any other task of any duration as a milestone by checking the **Mark task as milestone** check box available on the **Advanced** tab of the **Task Information** dialog box.

Example:

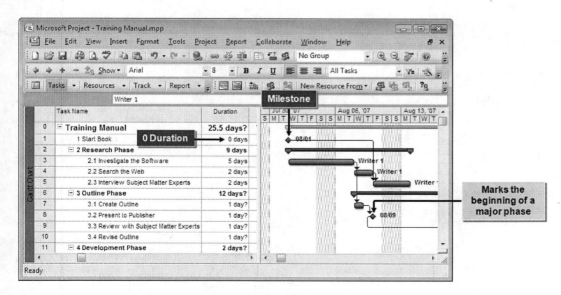

How to Enter the Task Duration Estimates

Procedure Reference: Enter the Task Duration Estimates

To enter the task duration estimates in your project plan:

1. Open the project plan in the **Gantt Chart** view.

2. In the task **Entry** table, select the **Duration** field for the task for which you wish to enter the duration.

3. Enter the duration for the tasks.

   - Type the desired number and press **Enter.**

   - Or, click the arrows to left of the text box.

4. If necessary, customize the duration.

   a. From the menu, choose **Tools→Options** to display the **Options** dialog box.

   b. Select the **Schedule** tab.

   c. In the **Scheduling options for [project]** section, select the **Duration is entered in** drop down list, to customize the desired duration unit for the project tasks.

ACTIVITY 2-4
Entering Task Duration Estimates

Data Files:

My Training Manual.mpp

Before You Begin:

1. The My Training Manual.mpp file is open.

2. Adjust the width of the **Task Name** column.

Scenario:

You compiled an estimate of the number of days each task in your project would take to accomplish. You need to provide this information against each of the tasks in the project.

What You Do	How You Do It
1. Enter the durations for Tasks 1 and 2.	a. In the **Entry** table, select the **Duration** field for the **Start Book** task.
	b. In the first row, in the **Duration** field, type *0* and press **Enter** to display the duration for the **Start Book** task in the **Gantt Chart.**
	c. Observe that in the **Gantt Chart** the symbol of a black diamond, ◆ is displayed against the **Start Book** task.
	d. In the second row, in the **Duration** column, type *9* and press **Enter** to display the duration of the **Research Phase** task.

2. **What are the screen changes that have occurred as a result of entering the task duration?**

3. Enter the task durations for the remaining tasks.

a. In the third row, in the **Duration** column, type *5* and press **Enter** to display the duration of the **Investigate the Software** task.

b. Enter the duration for the rest of the tasks as *2, 2, 5, 30, 5, 2, 3,* and *0* days.

c. Save the file.

TOPIC E
Add Resources in the Project Plan

You created tasks and assigned a duration to each of them. You need to determine who will perform the work to accomplish these assigned tasks. In this topic, you will add resources in the project plan.

If you plan to assign resources to tasks in your project plan, then you must enter resources into it. Without these resources, your project plan is simply a timeline of related tasks that theoretically will accomplish a goal. Furthermore, as your project gets underway, you may want to print reports that contain details of resource time and cost analysis.

Resources

Definition:

Resources are the people, equipment, material, and other miscellaneous items used to complete the tasks. A budget resource will include work, material, or cost resources. Once assigned to project tasks, resources determine the duration and the cost details for each task.

Example:

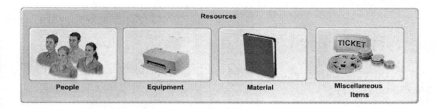

Resource Types

Project classifies resources into different types.

Type	Description
Work resources	Are the people or equipment. Example of work resources include the following: • Marjorie Westfall–An individual person. • Writer 1–A generic resource. • Editors–A group. • Fork Lift–A piece of equipment.

Type	Description
Material resources	Are the supplies or other consumable items used to complete tasks in a project. Examples of material resources include the following: • Paper–Material consumed while performing a task. • Ink • Raw material used for the manufacture of a product.
Cost resources	Are the miscellaneous expenses that vary from task to task and do not change by the amount of work performed on the task. Examples of cost resources include the following: • Airfare • Lodging
Budget resources	Are the work, material, and cost resource types. These capture the maximum capacity for a project to consume money, work, or material units. These resources can be applied only at the project level by assigning them to the project summary task.

Resource Sheet Fields

Information about resources can be maintained in a resource list, which can be created using the **Resource Sheet.**

Column Name	Description
ID	Contains an identifier number that Project automatically assigns to each resource.
Indicators	Displays icons that contain information about the resource.
Resource Name	Contains the name of the resource.
Type	Contains the resource type—**work, material,** or **cost.**
Material Label	Specifies the unit of measurement for a material resource. For example, steel can be measured in tons.
Initials	Specifies the resource name's abbreviation.
Group	Contains the name of the group that the resource belongs to—for example, external or internal resources.
Max. Units	Describes the percentage of work a resource can do when assigned to a task.
Std. Rate	Specifies the rate paid to the resource for regular and non-overtime work.
Ovt. Rate	Specifies the rate paid to the resource for overtime work.
Cost/Use	Specifies the cost that is accrued each time a resource is used.

Column Name	Description
Accrue At	Displays choices based on which costs, whether regular or overtime, will be calculated for a resource. This is either at the start or end of a task, or as a task is completed (prorated).
Base Calendar	Displays the calendar that is in use.
Code	Contains extra information about a resource.

The Resource Information Dialog Box

The **Resource Information** dialog box is used to enter, edit, and review information for selected resources in the project. The **Costs** tab displays options to enter, review, or change the cost information about the resource. On the **Notes** tab, you can enter or review the detailed notes about a specific resource. The **Custom Fields** tab allows you to enter and edit values for the resource's custom fields, if any.

How to Add Resources in the Project Plan

Procedure Reference: Enter Resources in the Resource Sheet

To enter resources in the **Resource Sheet:**

1. Open the project plan.
2. Display the **Resource Sheet** view.
   - Choose **View→Resource Sheet.**
   - In the **View Bar,** click the **Resource Sheet** icon.
   - Or, right-click the active pane indicator and choose **Resource Sheet.**
3. In the **Resource Entry** table, in the desired row, in the **Resource Name** field, type the resource name.
4. Press **Tab** to enter the resource and move to the **Type** field of the selected resource.
5. In the **Type** field, from the drop-down list, select the desired resource type and press **Tab** to move to the **Material Label** field.
6. If the resource is a material resource, in the **Material Label** field, enter the unit of measurement, and press **Tab** to move to the **Initials** field.
7. Enter the **Initials** of the resource.
   - In the **Initials** field, accept the default initials by pressing **Tab.**
   - Type the desired initials, and press **Tab.**
8. If necessary, if you wish to categorize the resources by group, in the **Group** field, type the group name, and press **Tab** to move to the **Max. Units** field.
9. Enter the maximum units that a resource can work on.
   - In the **Max. Units** field, type the desired **Unit.**
   - Or, in the **Max. Units** field, use the arrows to select the desired unit.
10. If necessary, make entries to the other fields.

Procedure Reference: Enter Resources using the Resource Information Dialog Box

To enter the resources using the **Resource Information** dialog box:

1. Open the desired project file and display the **Resource Sheet** view.
2. Display the **Resource Information** dialog box.
   - From the menu, choose **Project→Resource Information.**
   - In the **Resource Sheet** view, double-click anywhere on the desired row.
   - Or, on the keyboard, press **Shift+F2.**
3. On the **General** tab, enter the resource details and click **OK.**

Procedure Reference: Enter a Budget Resource in a Resource Sheet

To enter a budget resource in a **Resource Sheet:**

1. Display the **Resource Sheet** view.
2. In the **Resource Sheet,** enter all the necessary details about the resource.
3. If the resource is a budget resource, change the resource type.
   a. Display the **Resource Information** dialog box.
   b. On the **General** tab, check the **Budget** check box.
   c. Click **OK.**

Procedure Reference: Sort Resources in the Resource Sheet

To sort the resources displayed in the **Resource Sheet:**

1. Display the **Resource Sheet** view.
2. Display the **Sort** dialog box.
   - From the menu, choose **Project→Sort** to display the **Sort** submenu. On the displayed menu, choose the desired option.
   - Right-click the desired column heading and choose **Sort by.**
3. Set your sort criteria for sorting the resources.
   - In the **Sort** submenu, choose **by Cost, by Name,** or **by ID** to sort the resources by cost, name, or by their ID.
   - Choose **Sort by** and in the **Sort** dialog box, set your sort criteria.

 If you check the **Permanently renumber resources** check box in the **Sort** dialog box, your resources will not return to their original numbered order.

 You can also sort task and resource information in various views by displaying the desired view and choosing **Project→Sort.**

ACTIVITY 2-5

Entering Resources Using the Resource Sheet

Data Files:

My Training Manual.mpp

Before You Begin:

The My Training Manual.mpp file is open.

Scenario:

You created a list of people and material required to complete the tasks in your project. The amount spent on travel and funding for miscellaneous items have been identified too. You have also classified them into various categories and groups. The information needs to be captured in the project plan.

What You Do	How You Do It
1. Enter the **Writer 1, Editor 1, Project Manager 1,** and **Publisher** resources with their associated data.	a. Choose **View→Resource Sheet** to display the **Resource Sheet.**
	b. In the **Resource Entry** table, in the first row, in the **Resource Name** field, type **Writer 1** and press **Tab** to enter the resource name and move to the **Type** column of the selected resource.
	c. Observe that in the **Type** field, **Work** is already selected. Press **Tab** three times.
	d. In the first row, in the **Group** field, type **Internal** and press **Enter.**
	e. In the **Resource Entry** table, enter the following information:
	• **Resource Name:** *Editor 1*
	• **Type:** *Work*
	• **Group:** *Internal*
	• **Resource Name:** *Project Manager 1*
	• **Type:** *Work*
	• **Group:** *Internal*
	• **Resource Name:** *Publisher*
	• **Type:** *Work*
	• **Group:** *Internal*

2. Enter the rest of the resources with their associated data.

   a. In the **Resource Entry** table, in the fifth row, in the **Resource Name** field, type *Subject Matter Expert* and press **Tab** four times.

   b. In the fifth row, in the **Group** field, type *External* and press **Enter.**

   c. In the sixth row, in the **Resource Name** field, type *Travel Expenses* and press **Tab.**

   d. In the **Type** field, from the drop-down list, select **Cost** and press **Tab** three times.

   e. In the sixth row, in the **Group** field, type *Internal* and press **Enter.**

   f. In the seventh row, in the **Resource Name** field, type *Glossy Paper* and press **Tab.**

   g. In the **Type** field, from the drop-down list, select **Material** and press **Tab.**

   h. In the **Material Label** field, type *reams* and press **Tab** twice.

   i. In the seventh row, in the **Group** field, type *External* and press **Enter.**

3. Enter the budget resources.

a. In the 8th row, in the **Resource Name** field, type *Budget - Miscellaneous* and press **Tab.**

b. If necessary, adjust the width of the **Resource Name** column to view the resource names clearly.

c. In the **Type** field, from the drop-down list, select **Cost** and press **Tab** three times.

d. In the eighth row, in the **Group** field, type *Internal* and press **Enter.**

e. In the **Resource Entry** table, select the eighth row.

f. From the menu, choose **Project→ Resource Information** to launch the **Resource Information** dialog box.

g. On the **General** tab, check the **Budget** check box for the **Budget - Miscellaneous** resource.

h. Click **OK** to close the **Resource Information** dialog box.

i. In the **Resource Entry** table, enter the following budget resource information:

- **Resource Name:** *Budget - Labor*
- **Type:** *Work*
- **Group:** *Internal*
- **Resource Name:** *Budget - Material*
- **Type:** *Material*
- **Material Label:** *reams*
- **Group:** *Internal*

j. Save and close the file.

Lesson 2 Follow-up

In this lesson, you created a project plan. You also assigned a project calendar to the new project plan and entered various tasks including their durations into it. This will ensure that your project finishes on time, within budget, and within scope.

1. **What type of tasks will you use in your project plans?**

2. **When might you use milestone tasks in your project plans?**

3 | Managing Tasks in a Project Plan

Lesson Time: 1 hour(s), 20 minutes

Lesson Objectives:

In this lesson, you will manage tasks by organizing them and setting task relationships.

You will:

● Outline tasks in a project plan.

● Add a recurring task.

● Link dependent tasks.

● Set a constraint to a task.

● Set a task deadline.

● Add notes to a task.

Introduction

You now have a project plan that contains a complete list of project tasks and their durations. For Project to create a realistic schedule for these tasks, you will need to create relationships between the various tasks. In this lesson, you will manage your project plan by organizing tasks into more manageable pieces and forming relationships between them.

Managing all the tasks in a project plan file can be overwhelming, especially for large projects that involve many tasks. Project helps you manage these tasks by organizing them in a structure that shows how some tasks fit within broader groupings and how the tasks relate to one another. Doing this will make your project plan file easier to comprehend. Organizing tasks and creating task relationships are necessary steps in ensuring that Project will correctly calculate your project schedule.

TOPIC A
Outline Tasks

You entered your tasks along with their estimated duration in your project plan. Now you need to differentiate between the various tasks in the project plan by breaking them down into manageable chunks. In this topic, you will outline tasks by converting them to summary tasks or sub tasks.

As a project manager, you know that not all tasks are on the same level. Some tasks stand alone, while others are comprised of various other tasks. For example, you may have a summary task that requires many sub tasks to complete it. If you do not display the levels of tasks in an organized manner, it will be difficult to identify the hierarchical relationship between the summary task and the subtasks. You will also be unable to establish task relationships in a project as the priorities for the tasks will not be indicated in the project plan.

Work Breakdown Structure

Definition:

Work Breakdown Structure is a hierarchy of tasks in a project; it is represented by alphanumeric codes that identify the unique place of each task in the structure. Beginning with the project goal or objective, the project's work is progressively broken down until it reaches a level where you can estimate the duration of the lowest-level subtasks. The work breakdown structure can be drawn as a graphic that is displayed much like an organization chart with finite components, or it can be drawn as a simple outline.

Example:

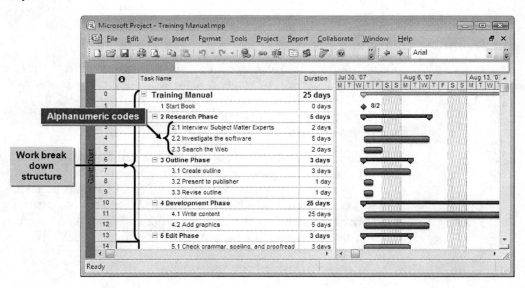

Outlining

Outlining allows you to organize the tasks in your plan into summary tasks and subtasks. Once you **Indent** the tasks to subtasks and **Outdent** the tasks as summary tasks, outlining assigns outline numbers that indicate the place of a task assignment in the project outline hierarchy. A task with an outline level of 1 is at the highest level in the outline, with no summary tasks above it. The number of outline levels you can set is unlimited for a task.

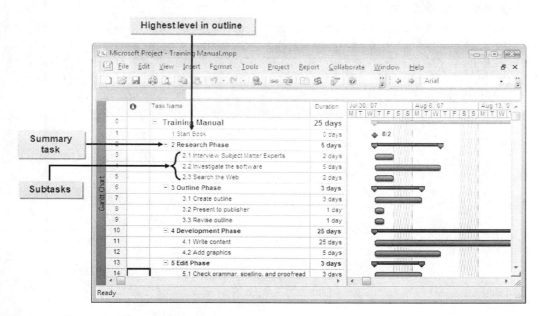

Figure 3-1: *Project with outline numbers.*

How to Outline Tasks

Procedure Reference: Outline Tasks

To outline tasks in the project plan:

1. In the **Gantt Chart** view, in the **Task Name** column, select a task or group of tasks.
2. On the **Formatting** toolbar, click a button to outline the tasks as subtask or summary task.
   - Click **Indent** to indent the task, making it a subtask.
   - Click **Outdent** to outdent the task, making it a summary task.
3. If necessary, collapse a summary task.
   - Click the (-) minus icon that appears to the left of the task you want to collapse.
   - Or, select the summary task, and on the **Formatting** toolbar, click **Hide Subtasks.**
4. If necessary, expand a summary task.
   - Click the (+) plus icon that appears to the left of the task name.
   - Or, select the summary task, and on the **Formatting** toolbar, click **Show Subtasks.**

Procedure Reference: Display Outline Numbers

To display the outline numbers:

1. Choose **Tools→Options.**

2. In the **Options** dialog box, select the **View** tab.

3. In the **Outline options for Outline** section, check the **Show outline number** check box.

4. Click **OK.**

5. If necessary, on the **Formatting** toolbar, from the **Show** drop-down list, select the desired outline level in which you want to display the tasks.

Summary tasks and Subtasks

Schedule and cost information from subtasks are accumulated at the summary task level. The start date of a summary task is determined by the earliest start date of any of its subtasks. Once a task is a summary task, you cannot edit the data related to that task. To display or hide the subtasks in your project plan, use the summary task's outline symbols, plus icon (+) and minus icon (-), which appear to the left of the task name.

ACTIVITY 3-1

Outlining Tasks in the Project Plan

Data Files:

Training Manual.mpp

Before You Begin:

From the C:\084774Data\Managing Tasks folder, open the Training Manual.mpp file.

Scenario:

While reviewing the project plan, you recognize that the tasks **Interview Subject Matter Experts, Investigate the Software,** and **Search the Web** can be grouped under the task **Research Phase.** You also want to see the hierarchy of the various tasks.

What You Do	How You Do It
1. Designate tasks as subtasks.	a. In the **Gantt Chart** view, in the **Task Name** column, click Task 3, and then hold down **Shift** and click Task 5.
	b. On the **Formatting** toolbar, click the **Indent** button. ⇨
2. Indent the remaining tasks in the project plan.	a. In the **Gantt Chart** view, in the **Task Name** column, select the Tasks 7, 8, and 9.
	b. On the **Formatting** toolbar, click the **Indent** button.
	c. Indent the remaining tasks under **Development Phase, Edit Phase, Review Phase** and **Print Phase.**
3. Display the outline numbers in your project plan to show the hierarchy of tasks.	a. Choose **Tools→Options.**
	b. In the **Options** dialog box, on the **View** tab, in the **Outline options for 'Training Manual.mpp'** section, check the **Show outline number** check box.
	c. Click **OK.**
	d. Click below Task 23 to observe that the outline numbers for each of the tasks are displayed in the project plan.

4. Display the summary tasks alone first and then all the tasks in the project plan.

a. On the **Formatting** toolbar, from the **Show** drop-down list, select **Outline Level 1** to display only the summary tasks.

b. From the **Show** drop-down list, select **All Subtasks** to display all the tasks in the project.

c. Save the file as *My Training Manual.mpp*

TOPIC B
Add a Recurring Task

You added tasks that occur only once throughout a project's life cycle. But there are some tasks, such as status meetings, which occur repeatedly at some particular time interval in the project plan. These tasks can occur multiple times throughout a project's life cycle. In this topic, you will add a recurring task.

Because project related meetings and check points can occur weekly, monthly, or at regular intervals throughout a project, Project allows you to designate these types of recurring events so that you do not have to enter them as separate tasks multiple times, and this can save you time and energy, as well as help eliminate errors.

Recurring Tasks

Definition:

A *recurring task* is a task that occurs repeatedly at regular intervals during the course of a project. Rather than entering these tasks multiple times, they can be entered once as a recurring task using the **Recurring Task Information** dialog box. A recurring task appears as a summary task with multiple sub tasks that represent each occurrence of the task. They are identified by the recurring task indicator icon, which appears to the left of the task in the **Indicators** column. A recurring task can be inserted in the project at any point in a project cycle.

Example:

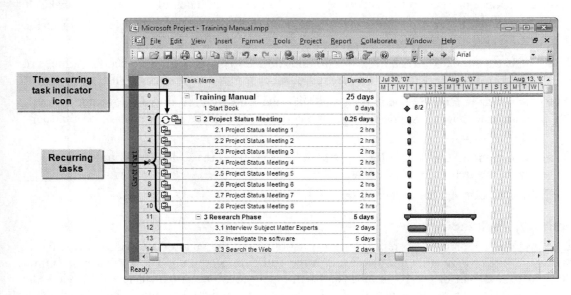

The Recurring Task Information Dialog Box

The **Recurring Task Information** dialog box helps you add a recurring task or review details about an existing recurring task. The recurring task names are entered in the **Task Name** text box and the recurrence pattern for the task is set by checking the desired options under the **Recurrence pattern** section, which sets the frequency of the task occurrence and the desired day. This dialog box also allows you to set the start date and the end date for a project under the **Range of recurrence** section and helps assign the desired calendar for scheduling the project from the **Calendar** drop-down list.

How to Add a Recurring Task

Procedure Reference: Add a Recurring Task

To add a recurring task:

1. Choose **View→Gantt Chart.**
2. In the **Task Name** column, select a row to insert the recurring task.
3. From the menu, choose **Insert→Recurring Task.**
4. In the **Recurring Task Information** dialog box, in the **Task Name** text box, type a name for the recurring task.
5. Double-click in the **Durations** text box and type the duration for which the task will occur.
6. In the **Recurrence pattern** section, check the desired options to set the frequency of occurrence and the day on which the task should recur.
7. In the **Range of recurrence** section, set the start and end dates of the recurring task.
   - Click the **Start** drop-down arrow and from the calendar that is displayed, select the start date for the recurring task.
   - Check the **End after** check box to end the recurring task after a specific number of occurrences, and specify the desired number in the **occurrences** spin box.
   - Check the **End by** check box, and click the **End by** drop-down arrow, and from the calendar that is displayed, select the end date to end the recurring task on that particular date.
8. In the **Calendar for scheduling this task** section, from the Calendar drop-down list, select the desired type of calendar.
9. Click **OK** to insert the recurring task.

Recurring Task Indicator

Project uses indicator icons to represent information about the state of a task, resource, or assignment. These indicators are displayed in the **Indicators** column. The **Indicators** column is located to the right of the ID number and will display various graphical icons. To view the important information associated with a task, resource, or assignment, place the mouse pointer over the icon. While various indicators exist, a recurring task is identified by the recurring task indicator.

ACTIVITY 3-2

Adding a Recurring Task

Data Files:

My Training Manual.mpp

Before You Begin:

The My Training Manual.mpp file is open.

Scenario:

You want to know the status of the project at regular intervals and so you wish to conduct a bi-weekly status meeting with the team on every other Tuesday for 2 hours. You also wish to specify a start date of August 07, 2007 and end the meeting by November 13, 2007 based on the assigned Our Global Company calendar. Now that you have the above specifications, you wish to incorporate the events to the project plan.

What You Do	How You Do It
1. Display the **Recurring Task Information** dialog box.	a. In the **Task Name** column, select Task 2.
	b. Choose **Insert→Recurring Task.**

2. Add a recurring task.

a. In the **Recurring Task Information** dialog box, in the **Task Name** text box, type *Project Status Meeting*

b. Double-click in the **Duration** text box and type *2 hrs*

c. In the **Recurrence pattern** section, observe that the **Weekly** option is selected by default.

d. In the **Recur every** text box, double-click and type *2* to set the task occurrence interval as bi-weekly.

e. Check the **Tuesday** check box to specify the day of the week on which the task should be scheduled.

f. In the **Range of recurrence** section, click the **Start** drop-down arrow.

g. From the calendar that is displayed, set the start date as August 07, 2007.

h. Click the **End by** drop-down arrow.

i. From the calendar that is displayed, set the end date as November 13, 2007.

j. In the **Calendar for scheduling this task** section, from the **Calendar** drop-down list, select **Our Global Company.**

k. Click **OK.**

3. Display screentips about the newly entered tasks.

a. In the **Indicators** column, place the mouse over the recurring task indicator, 🔄 to view the screentip that states, "This task occurs 7 times".

b. Save the file.

TOPIC C
Link Dependent Tasks

With your tasks organized as summary tasks and sub tasks, your project plan looks more manageable and readable. You are now ready to form relationships between the various dependent tasks. In this topic, you will link dependent tasks in a project.

Without relationships, all the tasks in your project will all be scheduled to begin on the project start date. For Project to determine a project time line or schedule, you must create relationships or links between the tasks. Without task relationships, you will not have a working project schedule.

Task Relationships

A task relationship or a dependency occurs when the starting time of a particular task is dependent on whether another task is starting or is completed and there are four kinds of dependencies.

Link Type	Description
Finish-to-Start (FS)	Task B cannot start until Task A finishes. For example, if you have two tasks, Lay Foundation and Pour Concrete, the Pour Concrete task cannot begin until the Lay Foundation task is complete.
Start-to-Start (SS)	Task B cannot start until Task A starts. The dependent task can begin anytime after the task that it depends on begins. The SS link type does not require both tasks to begin simultaneously. For example, if you have two tasks, Pour Concrete and Level Concrete, the Level Concrete task cannot begin until the Pour Concrete task begins.
Finish-to-Finish (FF)	Task B cannot finish until Task A finishes. The dependent task can be completed anytime after the task that it depends on is completed. The FF link type does not require that both tasks be completed simultaneously. For example, if you have two tasks, Finish Painting and Interior Designing, the Interior Designing task can be done only when the Finish painting task is completed.
Start-to-Finish (SF)	Task B cannot finish until task A starts. The dependent task can be completed anytime after the task it depends on begins. The SF link type does not require that the dependent task be completed concurrent with the beginning of the task on which it depends. For example, computer consultants must start installing software before they can finish testing computers.

Lag Time

Definition:

Lag time is a delay between two dependent tasks. In a project plan, a lag time adds waiting time after a task is completed. Lag time is set between a maximum of two tasks and it must be set after a dependency is created between those tasks. Lag time can be entered either as a duration or as a percentage of the duration of the predecessor task. Lag time is always entered as a positive value.

Example:

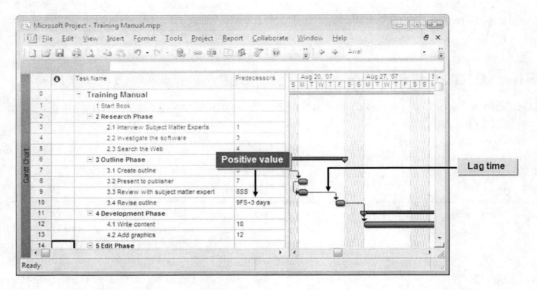

Lead Time

Definition:

Lead time is the overlap between two tasks that are linked by a dependency. In a project, lead time is set for tasks that can start when its predecessor task is half finished. It is entered either as a duration or as a percentage of the duration of the predecessor task. Lead time can be set between a maximum of two tasks and must be set after a dependency is created between those tasks. Lead time is always entered as a negative value.

Example:

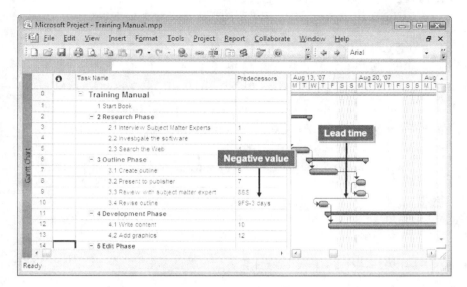

The Task Information Dialog Box

The **Task Information** dialog box is used to enter, review, or change information about a selected task. There are six tabs in this dialog box and each tab has different sections to view and change information about a task.

Tabs	*Description*
General	Used to enter durations of a task, track progress on a task by entering the percentage of completion, and to enter the start and finish date for a task. It is also used to hide a task bar and to roll up the subtasks to the summary task bar.
Predecessors	Used to enter a predecessor, set the predecessor type, and to enter the lag or lead time for a task.
Resources	Used to enter, review or change resource assignments, and assignment units for the selected task.
Advanced	Used to enter, review, or change additional task information for a task such as entering a deadline for task, change a constraint, and specify task type and task calendar.
Notes	Used to enter or review notes for a selected task.
Custom Fields	Used to view and assign values to custom task fields and outline codes.

How to Link Dependent Tasks

Procedure Reference: Link Dependent Tasks

To link dependent tasks in a project:

1. In the **Task Name** column, select two or more dependent tasks to be linked.
   - Hold down **Ctrl** and click the tasks to be linked to select nonadjacent tasks.
   - Hold down **Shift** and click the first and last task to be linked to select adjacent tasks.
2. On the **Standard** toolbar, click the **Link Tasks** button to create links between the selected tasks.
3. If necessary, on the **Standard** toolbar, click the **Unlink tasks** button to unlink the tasks.

Unlinking Tasks

The easiest way to unlink a task is to select the task and click the **Unlink tasks** button. This will remove all predecessor and successor links related to the task.

Procedure Reference: Add Lag or Lead Time

To add lag or lead time to a task:

1. Double-click the task for which you want to add lag or lead time.
2. In the **Task Information** dialog box, select the **Predecessors** tab.
3. In the **Lag** column, type the lead or lag time, either as a duration or as a percentage of the duration of the predecessor task.
   - In the **Lag** column, enter either a negative number or a negative value in percentage to set the lead time.
   - In the **Lag** column, enter either a positive number or a positive value in percentage to set the lag time.
4. Click **OK** and press **Enter.**

 Lag time can also be added by double-clicking the link on the **Gantt Chart.**

Procedure Reference: Change Task Predecessors

To change task predecessors:

1. In the **Task Name** column, double-click the task for which you need to change the predecessor.
2. In the **Task Information** dialog box, select the **Predecessors** tab.
3. Set a different task predecessor.
   - In the **Task Name** column, delete the predecessor displayed and enter a new predecessor.
   - Or, in the **Task Name** column, click the displayed predecessor to enable the predecessor drop-down arrow, and from the drop-down list, select the desired predecessor.
4. Click **OK.**

Procedure Reference: Modify Task Relationship Types

To modify task relationship types:

1. In the **Task Name** column, double-click the task for which you need to modify task relationship types.

2. In the **Task Information** dialog box, select the **Predecessor** tab.

3. In the **Type** column, click on the displayed type to enable the type drop-down arrow, and from the drop-down list that is displayed, select the desired type.

4. Click **OK.**

5. If necessary, on the **Standard** toolbar, click on the **Toolbar Options** and select the **Scroll to Task** button to display it.

ACTIVITY 3-3

Linking Tasks in a Project Plan

Data Files:

My Training Manual.mpp

Before You Begin:

1. The My Training Manual.mpp file is open.

2. In the **Task Name** column collapse the Project Status Meeting task and delete it.

3. On the **Standard** toolbar, click on the **Toolbar Options** and select the **Scroll to Task** button to display it.

4. Make the necessary arrangements in the data file to view the task name only and drag the divide bar of the **Gantt Chart** to the left.

Scenario:

Now that you have outlined your tasks, you want to form relationships between the various dependent tasks. You realize that you need to create a project time line and also want a systematic succession of the tasks, **Interview Subject Matter Expert, Investigate the Software,** and **Search the Web.** You need to set dependencies between **Start Book** and **Interview Subject Matter Expert** and form a relationship between all milestones and subtasks in the project.

What You Do	How You Do It
1. Form a link between the dependent tasks.	a. In the **Task Name** column, select Tasks 3, 4, and 5.
	b. In the **Gantt Chart,** observe that the Gantt bars of the tasks are unlinked.
	c. On the **Standard** toolbar, click the **Link Tasks** button.
	d. In the **Gantt Chart,** observe that the Gantt bars of the selected tasks are linked.
2. Establish a link between the tasks **Start Book** and **Investigate the Software.**	a. In the **Task Name** column, select Task 1 and hold down **Ctrl** and select Task 3.
	b. On the **Standard** toolbar, click the **Link Tasks** button.
	c. In the **Gantt Chart,** observe that the Gantt bars of the selected tasks are linked.

3. Link the remaining subtasks.

    a. Select the Tasks 5, 7, 8, and 9 and click the **Link Tasks** button to link the tasks.

    b. Link the Tasks 9, 11, and 12; 12, 14 and 15; 15, 17, and 18; 18, 20, 21, and 22; 22 and 23 to complete the file.

    c. Save the file.

ACTIVITY 3-4
Modifying a Task Relationship Type

Data Files:

My Training Manual.mpp

Before You Begin:

1. The My Training Manual.mpp file is open.

2. Drag the divide bar to the right till the **Predecessors** column is visible.

Scenario:

In your project plan, you realize that a task to review the outline with the subject matter expert is missing and needs to be added. You also know that this new task cannot start until its predecessor, Task 8, starts. You need to update the project plan to reflect these changes.

What You Do	How You Do It
1. Add a subtask to the **Outline Phase** summary task.	a. Select Task 9 and press **Insert** to insert a new task.
	b. In the inserted row, in the **Task Name** column, type **Review with Subject Matter Expert** and in the **Duration** column type **1 day** and press **Enter.**
	c. Select Task 9.
2. View the Gantt bar for the tasks **Review with Subject Matter Expert** and **Present to Publisher** displaying the new relationship.	a. Double-click on Task 9 to display the **Task Information** dialog box.
	b. Select the **Predecessors** tab.
	c. Observe that the predecessor is **Present to Publisher** and the relationship type is **Finish-to-Start (FS).**

3. Change the task relationship type for the task **Review with Subject Matter Expert** to start-to-start.

a. In the **Task Information** dialog box in the **Predecessors** tab, click in the **Type** column for the task **Present to Publisher.**

b. From the **Type** drop-down list for the task, **Present to Publisher** and select **Start-to-Start (SS).**

c. Click **OK.**

d. Scroll to the right and observe that the Gantt bar for the Tasks 8 and 9 show that they both start on the same day.

e. Save the file.

ACTIVITY 3-5
Adding Lead Time to a Task

Data Files:

My Training Manual.mpp

Before You Begin:

The My Training Manual.mpp file is open.

Scenario:

As a project manager, you are always looking for ways to save time and money. Since the editor can begin editing the manual before all the graphics are added, you decide to set a lead time to the task **Check Grammar, Spelling, and Proofread.**

What You Do	How You Do It
1. View the default lag time for Task 15.	a. Double-click Task 15.
	b. In the **Lag** column of the **Add Graphics** task, observe that **0d** is displayed indicating that the lag time is set to zero days by default.
2. Set 50 percent lead time for Task 15.	a. In the **Lag** field, click, type *—50%* and press **Enter.**
	b. Click **OK.**
	c. If necessary, click and drag the divide bar until you view the **Predecessors** column.
	d. Select the **Predecessors** column of Task 15.
	e. In the **Gantt Chart** view, scroll to the right to view the Gantt bars of the selected tasks.
	f. Observe that the **Predecessors** column displays the lead time, and the Gantt bars for the Tasks 13 and 15 overlap reflecting the new relationship with –50% as the lead time.
	g. Save the file.

TOPIC D
Set a Constraint to a Task

You formed links between tasks in your project plan, which in turn, schedules start and finish dates for each project task. Having managed projects, you know how likely it is that other factors, such as personnel availability, will affect the actual start or finish dates of tasks. In this topic, you will set a constraint to a task to account for these factors.

Suppose you have a computer consultant who must install software for your project and is not available until after a specific date. This task will be a constraint for other dependent tasks to be completed or started at their scheduled time. In such a situation, you may not want to have Project automatically calculate all your tasks' start and finish dates. To deal with these various factors, or constraints, Project allows you to set task constraints so that the project schedule is recalculated based on the constraint.

Constraints

Definition:

Constraints are conditions or limitations placed on the start or finish date of a task in a project plan. Task constraints affect the project schedule and may also affect the overall project duration. When you set a project using a start date, by default, all tasks are scheduled to start with an **As Soon As Possible** constraint. If the project is set using a finish date, tasks are scheduled to start with an **As Late As Possible** constraint. When a constraint is set for a task, an icon is displayed in the Indicators column to the left of the task.

Example:

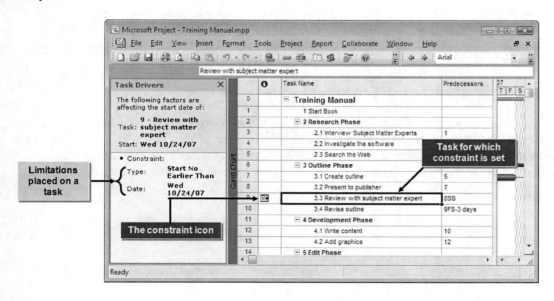

Task Constraint Types

There are different types of constraints with various degrees of flexibility.

Constraint Type	Description
As Soon As Possible	The task is scheduled to start as soon as possible, based on other constraints and relationships in the project. This is the default constraint in a project scheduled from the start date. It is the most flexible constraint.
As Late As Possible	The task is scheduled to finish as late as possible, based on other constraints and relationships in the project. This is the default constraint in a project scheduled from the finish date. It is a flexible constraint.
Start No Earlier Than	The task must be scheduled to start on the specified date or later. It is a less flexible constraint.
Start No Later Than	The task must be scheduled to start on the specified date or sooner. It is a less flexible constraint.
Finish No Earlier Than	The task must be scheduled to finish on the specified date or later. It is a less flexible constraint.
Finish No Later Than	The task must be scheduled to finish on the specified date or sooner. It is a less flexible constraint.
Must Start On	The task must be scheduled to start on the specified date. It is the least flexible constraint.
Must Finish On	The task must be scheduled to finish on the specified date. It is the least flexible constraint.

The Task Drivers Pane

The **Task Drivers** pane displayed to the left of the **Gantt Chart** provides information on factors affecting the start date of the selected tasks. If the selected task has a constraint, the **Task Drivers** pane displays the type of constraint that is currently placed on the task, including the date associated with the constraint. The **Task Drivers** pane is not displayed by default, it can be accessed from the **Project** menu.

How to Apply a Constraint to a Task

Procedure Reference: Apply a Constraint to a Task

To apply a constraint to a task:

1. Double-click the task for which you need to apply a constraint.

2. In the **Task Information** dialog box, select the **Advanced** tab.

3. Click the **Constraint type** drop-down arrow to display the drop-down list.

4. From the drop-down list, select the desired type of constraint.

5. Click the **Constraint date** drop-down arrow to display the calendar and from the calendar that is displayed, select the desired date.

6. Click **OK.**

Date Constraints

If tasks change, causing you to miss a deadline, a constraint causes a warning message box to be displayed. You can also change the way Project honors task constraints. If you want Project to note the conflict, without considering it when creating the project schedule, choose **Tools→ Options**, select the **Schedule** tab, and uncheck the **Task will always honor their constraint dates** checkbox.

ACTIVITY 3-6

Setting a Constraint to a Task

Data Files:

My Training Manual.mpp

Before You Begin:

The My Training Manual.mpp file is open.

Scenario:

As per your project schedule, the writer must meet with the subject matter expert to review the outline at the earliest. Recently, you received the information that the subject matter expert would not be available as scheduled and therefore the task has to be postponed. As there are factors affecting this task, you also wish to keep track of this inflexible factor.

What You Do	How You Do It
1. Set the date constraint for Task 9.	a. Double-click Task 9.
	b. In the **Task Information** dialog box, select the **Advanced** tab.
	c. In the **Constrain task** section, from the **Constraint type** drop-down list, select **Start No Earlier Than.**
	d. From the **Constraint date** drop-down calendar, select the constraint date as **August 20, 2007.**
	e. Click **OK.**
	f. Click Task 9.
	g. Place the mouse pointer over the constraint icon, ▦ in the **Indicators** column to view that August 20 has been set as the constraint date.
2. Display the **Task Drivers** pane to view the factors affecting Task 9.	a. Choose **Project→Task Drivers.**
	b. Observe that the **Task Drivers** pane on the left displays the **Constraint Type** as **Start No Earlier Than** and **Constraint Date** as **Mon 8/20/07.**
	c. Save the file.

TOPIC E
Set a Task Deadline

You set a task constraint, which forced Project to recalculate the project schedule. Because these constraints limit Project's ability to reschedule tasks, you need to ensure that you set a target completion date for a task that does not affect the project's schedule and end date. In this topic, you will set a task deadline.

Setting constraints restricts Microsoft Project's ability to reschedule tasks. Using an alternative can help alleviate scheduling issues. Setting a deadline for a task helps to complete the task as targeted without having Project actually alter your schedule.

Deadline

Deadline is a target date that indicates when you want a task to be completed. If the deadline date passes and the task is incomplete, Project displays a downward pointing arrow as an indicator in the **Gantt Chart.** Unlike a constraint, a deadline does not affect project scheduling unless you are scheduling from the project finish date and applying an **As Late As Possible** constraint.

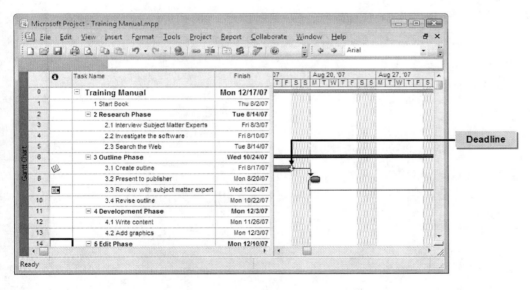

Figure 3-2: *Project displays a downward pointing arrow as a deadline.*

How to Set a Task Deadline

Procedure Reference: Set a Task Deadline

To set a task deadline:

1. Double-click the task for which you want to set the deadline.

2. In the **Task Information** dialog box, select the **Advanced** tab.

3. In the **Constrain task** section, click the **Deadline** drop-down arrow and from the calendar that is displayed, select the finish date for the task.

4. Click **OK** to insert the deadline.

ACTIVITY 3-7
Setting a Task Deadline

Data Files:

My Training Manual.mpp

Before You Begin:

1. The My Training Manual.mpp file is open.

2. Close the **Task Drivers** pane.

Scenario:

As a project manager, you need to ensure that all tasks are completed according to plan because completing the course as scheduled is the key to the success of the project. In order to achieve the target, you need to ensure that the task, **Create Outline** is completed as scheduled as it is the most crucial phase in the project and this needs to be reflected in the project plan.

What You Do	How You Do It
1. Set a deadline for Task 7.	a. Double-click Task 7.
	b. On the **Advanced** tab, in the **Constrain task** section, from the **Deadline** drop-down calendar, set the date to August 15, 2007.
	c. Click **OK** to set the deadline date.
2. Display screentip for the deadline in the **Gantt Chart.**	a. In the **Gantt Chart,** on the Gantt bar for Task 7, place the mouse pointer over the downward pointing white arrow, and view the screentip for the task displaying the deadline.
	b. Save the file.

TOPIC F
Add Notes to a Task

After organizing tasks and establishing task relationships, you have more or less captured data related to tasks in your project plan. However, you might need to flag some information relevant to a task that may come of use or function as a reminder note. In this topic, you will add such information, in the form of notes, to a task.

If you have a task on an interview with specialist, you might need to mark some crucial information with respect to the task, somewhere in the project plan. For instance, your client might want transcripts of the interview in a CD format. Adding a note that reminds you to deliver the CD at the end of the task, will ensure that you do not miss the deliverable. Microsoft Project will help you create and track task notes during the project.

Task Notes

Task notes are additional or supporting information that is added to a task. You can add notes to record specifications, customer requirements, quality measures, or any general information related to a task. Project also offers the flexibility to attach related documents, including Microsoft Word or Microsoft Excel files, or to create hyperlinks to supporting information. Notes can also be formatted as desired.

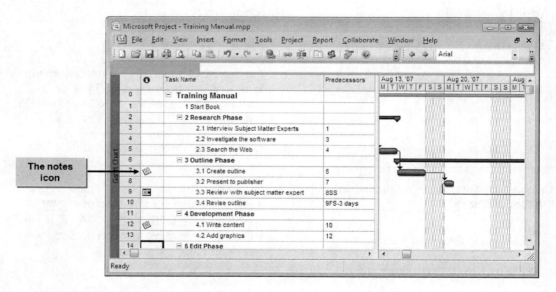

Figure 3-3: *Project with notes added to tasks.*

How to Add Notes to a Task

Procedure Reference: Add Notes to a Task

To add notes to a task:

1. Select the desired sheet view to add the notes.

    ● From the **View** menu, choose **Task Usage** to display the **Task Usage** sheet view.

    ● From the **View** menu, choose **Resource Sheet** to display the **Resource Sheet** sheet view.

    ● From the **View** menu, choose **Resource Usage** to display the **Resource Usage** sheet view.

2. In the selected sheet view, select a task to which you want to add a note.

3. From the **Project** menu, choose the desired note.

    ● Choose **Task Notes** to add a task note.

    ● Or, choose **Resource Notes** to add a resource note.

    ● Or, choose **Assignment Notes** to add an assignment note.

4. Click in the **Notes** text area to enter the desired note.

5. Click **OK** to insert the desired notes.

Procedure Reference: Format Notes

To format notes in a project:

1. Select the desired sheet view.

2. Double-click the task with the note you want to format.

3. In the **Notes** tab, in the **Notes** text area, select the note in the text area.

4. In the **Notes** section, click a button to apply the desired formatting to the selected note.

    ● Click the **Format Font** button to display the **Font** dialog box, and choose the desired option to change the font.

    ● Click the **Align Left** button to align notes on the left side.

    ● Click **Center** to align notes to the center.

    ● Click the **Align Right** button to align notes to the right.

    ● Click the **Bulleted List** button to display the note as a bulleted list.

    ● Click the **Insert Object** button to display the **Insert Object** dialog box, and choose the desired option to insert an object to the note.

5. Click **OK** to format the note.

ACTIVITY 3-8
Adding Notes to a Task

Data Files:

My Training Manual.mpp

Before You Begin:

The My Training Manual.mpp file is open.

Scenario:

As a project manager, you have too many functions associated with a task. You want to keep track of these additional functions, which are crucial to a task. You want to be reminded of sending the outline.doc to the Marketing department for the task **Create Outline,** based on the storyboard, to insert graphics for the content for the task **Add Graphics** and providing a hard copy proof to the project manager for the task **Print Proof.** You want to flag the above specifications in the project plan.

What You Do	How You Do It
1. Add notes to tasks, **Create Outline, Add Graphics**, and **Print Proof**.	a. In the **Task Name** column, double-click Task 7 to display the **Task Information** dialog box.
	b. Select the **Notes** tab.
	c. In the **Notes** text area, type *Send Outline.doc to the marketing department.*
	d. Click **OK** to insert the note.
	e. Double-click Task 13 and in the **Notes** text area, type *Based on the storyboard, insert appropriate graphics for the content.*
	f. Click **OK** to insert the note.
	g. Double-click Task 21 and in the **Notes** text area, type *Provide a hard copy proof to the project manager.*
	h. Click **OK** to insert the note.

2. Display the screentip for the **Notes** indicator for the task **Create Outline.**

a. Click Task 7.

b. In the Indicators column, for Task 7, place the mouse pointer over the notes indicator icon, [icon] to view the notes message for the task.

c. Save and close the file.

Handwritten notes:

• PROJECT | WBS | DEFINE CODE : CREATE | MODIFY OUTLINE STRUCTURE

LEAD TIME ENTERED AS NEGATIVE LAG TIME

LEAD TIME = 5 DAYS
ENTER -5 FOR LAG TIME.
-50%

• TRY TO AVOID CONSTRAINTS - ALLOW LEAD || LAG
TIME TO WORK.

p. 61
p. 72

Lesson 3 Follow-up

In this lesson, you managed tasks by organizing them and setting task relationships. This helped you schedule the project timeline for each task which in turn will ensure that the project is completed as scheduled.

1. **When might you set a deadline in your project plan?**

2. **What type of task relationships might you use?**

4 Managing Resources in a Project Plan

Lesson Time: 1 hour(s), 30 minutes

Lesson Objectives:

In this lesson, you will manage resources in a project plan.

You will:

- Create a resource calendar.
- Assign resources to tasks.
- Assign additional resources to a task.
- Enter associated costs for resources in the project plan.
- Enter values for budget resources.
- Resolve resource conflicts.

Introduction

You organized tasks in your project plan. Now, for your project to get underway, you will need resources to perform the necessary work to complete these tasks. In this lesson, you will manage the resources who will perform the project tasks.

If you create a to-do list without identifying who will perform the necessary work to complete the items, it is likely that the items on the list will not get accomplished. Similarly, if you want to use Project to track the amount of work done and/or the amount of materials used in completing a project, you will have to use resources in your project plan file. Managing resources also enables the calculation of a more accurate schedule of the duration of each task.

TOPIC A

Create a Resource Calendar

You entered resource information into the project plan, and assigned a project calendar to each work resource. Perhaps, some resource schedules are different from the project calendar and you need to account for these differences. In this topic, you will create a resource calendar.

For Project to correctly schedule resources to work on tasks, you must create and assign a resource calendar for those resources that do not work for the hours specified in the project calendar. Perhaps, you have a resource who works part-time. If you neglect to create a different calendar for this employee, your schedule will be incorrect because it will allocate the resource for an 8-hour day, instead of a 4-hour day.

How to Create a Resource Calendar

Procedure Reference: Create a Resource Calendar

To create a resource calendar:

1. Display the **Resource Sheet** view.
2. Double-click the resource for which you need to create a resource calendar.
3. In the **Resource Information** dialog box, on the **General** tab, click **Change Working Time.**
4. In the **Change Working Time** dialog box, make the necessary working time edits to the resource calendar information.
5. Click **OK** to save the changes.
6. In the **Resource Information** dialog box, click **OK.**

 You can also change the resource calendar information in the **Change Working Time** dialog box by choosing **Tools→Change Working Time.**

ACTIVITY 4-1

Creating a Resource Calendar

Data Files:

Training Manual.mpp

Before You Begin:

From the C:\084774Data\Managing Resources folder, open the Training Manual.mpp file.

Scenario:

You have just been told that, as of today, the resource, Staff Assistant 2 is changing her employment status to part-time. To accommodate this change of status, you need to change her working hours in the project plan. You know that the working hours are Monday to Friday, from 8:00 A.M.–12:00 P.M. Additionally, the resource is only available to work on the project from October 15, 2007 through November 30, 2007.

What You Do	How You Do It
1. Display the **Change Working Time** dialog box for the resource, **Staff Assistant 2.**	a. Choose **View→Resource Sheet.**
	b. In the **Resource Name** column, double-click Resource 9, **Staff Assistant 2,** to display the **Resource Information** dialog box.
	c. On the **General** tab, click **Change Working Time** to display the **Change Working Time** dialog box.

2. Alter the calendar to reflect an 8:00 A.M.—12:00 P.M. work schedule, Monday through Friday.

    a. In the **Change Working Time** dialog box, in the **Click on a day to see its working times** calendar preview, scroll down to **October 2007** and select **15.**

    b. Select the **Work Weeks** tab.

    c. Verify that the **[Default]** working time row is selected and click **Details.**

    d. In the **Details for '[Default]'** dialog box, in the **Select day(s)** list box, notice that **Monday** is selected by default. Hold down **Shift** and then click **Friday** to select the **Monday** to **Friday** working week.

    e. Select the **Set day(s) to these specific working times** option to set the new timings for **Staff Assistant 2.**

    f. In the second row, select the **From** field and press **Delete** to delete the afternoon working hours from **1:00 PM** to **5:00 PM.**

    g. In the **Details for '[Default]'** dialog box, click **OK** to close it.

    h. In the **Change Working Time** dialog box, click **OK** to close it.

3. Modify the dates for which the resource, **Staff Assistant 2,** is available.

    a. In the **Resource Information** dialog box, in the **Resource Availability** section, in the first row, select the **Available From** field and type *10-15-2007*

    b. In the first row, in the **Available To** field, click and type *11-30-2007*

4. Add a note to the resource, **Staff Assistant 2.**

    a. In the **Resource Information** dialog box, select the **Notes** tab.

    b. In the **Notes** text box, click and type *Given enough notice, this resource can work afternoons instead of mornings.*

    c. Click **OK** to add the note to the resource and to close the **Resource Information** dialog box.

    d. Save the file as *My Training Manual.mpp*

TOPIC B
Assign Resources to Tasks

You created a calendar for a resource that works in a different schedule. With resources entered and resource calendars decided, you are ready for the next step in the creation of your project plan. In this topic, you will assign resources to the tasks in your project plan.

Imagine a project plan where none of its team members know what their responsibilities are. Words such as chaos and confusion may come to mind. To identify who is responsible for completing the tasks in your project plan, you need to assign resources to these tasks. By assigning resources, you allow Project to accurately schedule tasks using the resource calendars and assignment units information. Furthermore, to have Project help you in accounting for resource time and costs, you will need to assign resources to project tasks.

Part-Time Resources

A *part-time resource* is scheduled to work less than 40 hours in a work week. Normally, in a project, full-time resources are scheduled to work 100 percent of their calendar time on that task. In Microsoft Project, this information is registered in the **Units** field in various views. If you need to assign resources to work less than 100 percent of their time on a task, you can alter the information in the **Units** field by entering the correct percentage.

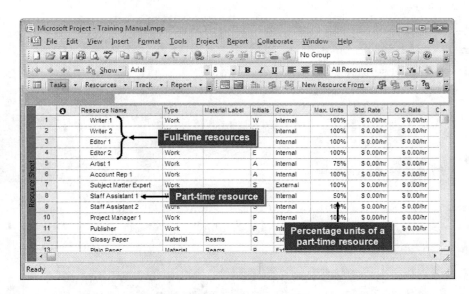

Figure 4-1: *Part-time resources work less than 100 percent of their calendar time on a task.*

Combination View

When you want to display two views simultaneously, you can use the *combination view*. The view at the bottom pane of the combination view shows detailed information about the data selected in the top pane.

The Task Form

The **Task Form** is a Project view that displays a form for entering and editing information about a task. It is displayed by default in the bottom pane of the combination view. When used in a combination view, the **Task Form** can be very helpful, allowing you to display, enter, or edit the detailed information for a selected task. The **Previous** and **Next** buttons can be used to move forward and backward through a task list.

How to Assign Resources to Tasks

Procedure Reference: Assign Resources to Tasks Using the Assign Resources Dialog Box

To assign resources to tasks using the **Assign Resources** dialog box:

1. Display the **Gantt Chart** view.

2. In the task **Entry** table, in the desired row, in the **Task Name** field, select the desired task for which you want to assign a resource.

3. Display the **Assign Resources** dialog box.

    ● From the menu, choose **Tools→Assign Resources.**

    ● On the **Standard** toolbar, click the **Assign Resources** button.

    ● Or, on the keyboard, press **Alt+F10.**

4. In the **Resources** section, in the **Resource Name** field, select the resource(s) that you want to assign.

To select multiple resources, press **Ctrl.**

5. Click **Assign**. A check mark will appear next to the resource name.

6. If necessary, assign resources for other tasks within your project plan.

7. When finished, click **Close.**

To remove an assigned resource, display the **Assign Resources** dialog box, select the resource to remove, and then click **Remove.**

Procedure Reference: Assign Resources Using the Task Entry Table

To assign resources using the task **Entry** table:

1. Display the **Gantt Chart** view.

2. Drag the divide bar to the right so that the **Resource Names** column is displayed.

3. In the task **Entry** table, in the desired row, in the **Resource Names** field, select the task for which you want to assign a resource to.

4. From the required task's **Resource Names** drop-down list, select the desired resource and press **Enter.**

Procedure Reference: Assign Resources Using the Task Information Dialog Box

To assign resources using the **Task Information** dialog box:

1. Display the **Gantt Chart** or the **Task Usage** view.
2. Select the desired task and display the **Task Information** dialog box.
3. Select the **Resources** tab.
4. In the **Resources** section, assign the desired resource to the task.
   - In the **Resource Name** column, select the desired cell and type the desired resource name.
   - Or, in the **Resource Name** column, from the desired cell's drop-down list, select the desired resource name.
5. Click **OK.**

Procedure Reference: Display a Combination View

To display a combination view:

1. Choose **Window→Split.**
2. Click anywhere in the bottom pane to activate the view. The active view bar indicates the pane that is active.
3. From the **View** menu, choose the desired view that should appear in the bottom pane.

 To close the combination view, choose **Window→Remove Split.**

Procedure Reference: Assign Resources to Tasks Using the Task Form View

To assign resources to tasks using the **Task Form** view:

1. Display the **Task Form** view.
2. In the **Task Form,** in the **Resource Name** column, assign the resources to the task.
3. If necessary, for a work resource, check the **Effort driven** check box to calculate the cost based on the effort and press **Enter.**
4. If necessary, click the **Previous** or **Next** buttons to navigate to other tasks and add resources to them.

ACTIVITY 4-2

Assigning Resources to a Task

Data Files:

My Training Manual.mpp

Before You Begin:

The My Training Manual.mpp file is open.

Scenario:

After entering the tasks and the list of resources, you would like to link the resources with their designated tasks. You want to view both the list of tasks and the individual task's description in the same window when you link the resources to the tasks. Also, as the manager of your project, you have the additional responsibility of presenting the outline to the publisher and you would like to add yourself as a part time resource for task 8, **Present to Publisher.**

What You Do	How You Do It
1. Display the combination view with the **Gantt Chart** in the top pane.	a. On the extreme left of the application window, right-click the active pane indicator and choose **Gantt Chart.**
	b. Drag the divide bar to the far right of the screen, so that all fields in the task **Entry** table are visible.
	c. Choose **Window→Split.**

2. Assign a resource to Task 3.

    a. In the **Gantt Chart** view, select Task 3, **Investigate the Software.**

    b. On the **Standard** toolbar, click the **Assign Resources** button.

    c. If necessary, drag the **Assign Resources** dialog box to the bottom left corner of the window, so that you can see all of the **Task Form** information.

    d. Scroll down and select **Writer 1.**

    e. Click **Assign.**

    f. Click **Close** to close the **Assign Resources** dialog box.

    g. Observe that in the task **Entry** table, in the **Resource Names** field, **Writer 1** is listed for task 3, **Investigate the Software.**

3. Assign resources to Tasks 4, 5, and 7.

    a. In the task **Entry** table, select the **Resource Names** field for Task 4, **Search the Web.**

    b. In the **Resource Names** field, in the drop-down list, scroll down and select **Writer 1** and press **Enter** to assign the resource to the task.

    c. In the **Resource Names** field, in the drop-down list for Task 5, scroll down and select **Writer 1** and press **Enter.**

    d. In the **Task Form** view, click **Next.**

    e. In the **Task Form** view, in the first row, in the **Resource Name** field, in the drop-down list, scroll down and select **Writer 1.**

    f. In the **Task Form** view, click **OK** to assign the resource to the task.

4. Assign **Project Manager 1** to work part-time on Task 8.

a. In the **Task Form** view, click **Next** to move to Task 8, **Present to Publisher.**

b. In the **Task Form** view, in the first row, in the **Resource Name** drop-down list, scroll down and select **Project Manager 1.**

c. In the first row, in the **Units** field, click and type *50%* and click **OK.**

d. In the **Gantt Chart** view, widen the **Resource Names** column and observe that the 50 percent value is indicated in square parenthesis after the **Project Manager 1** resource.

e. In the **Task Form** view, in the **Work** column, observe that the value is 4 hours to indicate that the **Project Manager 1** resource is scheduled to work only for 4 hours on Task 8.

f. Save the file.

TOPIC C
Assign Additional Resources to a Task

You assigned the resources for your tasks. Critical tasks in your project may need additional efforts. In this topic, you will assign additional resources to tasks in your project plan.

Knowing how to assign more than one resource to tasks within your project plan is a necessary skill if, in fact, tasks in your project plan require multiple resources. Neglecting to assign multiple resources, where necessary, can result in overallocated resources and stressed out team members. It is also equally important that you, the project manager, understand how Project calculates duration, work, and units with regard to resource assignments. If you do not have this knowledge, your project schedule may be incorrectly calculated.

Effort-Driven Scheduling

When you assign resources to a task, Project shortens the task duration and when you remove resources from a task, Project lengthens the task duration. This is called effort-driven scheduling. It does not, however, change the total work for the task. By default, all tasks are marked **Effort driven.**

Task Types

You can control the way your task schedule is managed by selecting task types. By using task types, you can make one of the following three variables—duration, work, or units— unchangeable in scheduling calculations. Setting any of the three task variables as fixed provides an extra measure of control over the project schedule. Since the duration of each task is determined by the formula Duration = Work / Units, you can choose that part of the equation that Project calculates by setting the **Task type.**

You can set any of the three task variables as fixed using the **Task type** drop-down list.

Task Type	Description
Fixed Units	A task with a fixed unit value. This is the default **Task type.** Assigning additional resources to a task reduces the task's duration. For example, if one resource is assigned to complete the task of stuffing envelopes, adding another resource will shorten this task's duration.
Fixed Duration	A task with a fixed value of duration. Any changes made to the work or to the assigned resources does not impact the task's duration. Assigning additional resources to this task type decreases the individual unit values for resources. For example, if a delivery is made from one site to another and only one truck is necessary to complete the task, assigning additional resources to the task does not decrease the task's duration.

Task Type	Description
Fixed Work	A task in which the amount of work to be completed is fixed. If changes are made to the task's duration or to the number of assigned resources, there is no impact on work. Assigning additional resources shortens the duration of the task for this task type. If a task has a task type of **Fixed Work,** you cannot change the **Effort driven** setting for that task.

How to Assign Additional Resources to a Task

Procedure Reference: Change a Task Type

To change the type of a task:

1. Display the **Gantt Chart** view.
2. Double-click the desired task to display the **Task Information** dialog box.
3. On the **Advanced** tab, from the **Task type** drop-down list, select the task type that you want to set and click **OK.**

 You can also change the type of a task by using the **Task type** drop-down list in the **Task Form.**

Adding Effort-Driven Component to Tasks

An effort-driven schedule is set based on the nature of task. Adding an effort-driven component to a task increases or decreases the effort involved in the particular task. For each task, the task type is set based on the variable that is a constant or on the one you want to control as a project manager.

Procedure Reference: Change the Effort-Driven Scheduling for a Task

To change the effort-driven scheduling for a task:

1. Display the **Gantt Chart** view.
2. Double-click the desired task. In the **Task Information** dialog box, select the **Advanced** tab.
3. Uncheck the **Effort driven** check box and click **OK.**

Procedure Reference: Assign Additional Resources to a Task Using the Task Information Dialog Box

To assign additional resources to a task using the **Task Information** dialog box:

1. Display the **Gantt Chart** view.
2. Double-click the desired task. In the **Task Information** dialog box, select the **Resources** tab.
3. In the **Resources** section, in the desired row, in the **Resource Name** column, enter the desired resource name and press **Enter.**
4. Click **OK** to close the **Task Information** dialog box.

Procedure Reference: Assign an Additional Resource Using the Assign Resources Dialog Box

To assign additional resources to tasks using the **Assign Resources** dialog box:

1. Display the **Gantt Chart** view.
2. In the task **Entry** table, select the **Task Name** column for the task that you want to assign an additional resource to.
3. Display the **Assign Resources** dialog box.
4. In the **Resource Name** column, select the resource that you want to assign.
5. Click **Assign.**
6. When finished, click **Close.**

 If the assigned resource's work is not effort driven, you can undo the assigning of a resource to a task by clicking **Undo Entry** on the **Standard** toolbar.

Procedure Reference: Assign Additional Resources to a Task Using Task Form

To assign additional resources to a task using **Task Form:**

1. Display the **Task Form** view.
2. Use the **Previous** and **Next** buttons to navigate to the desired task.
3. In the desired row, in the **Resource Name** column, select a resource.
4. In the **Task Form** view, click **OK.**

Procedure Reference: Assign an Additional Resource Using the Task Entry Table

To assign additional resources to tasks using the task **Entry** table:

1. Display the **Gantt Chart.**
2. In the task **Entry** table, select the **Resource Name** column for the task that you want to assign an additional resource to.
3. Display the **Resource Name** drop-down list and type comma to indicate that an additional resource is to be added.
4. From the **Resource Name** drop-down list, select the additional resource name and press **Enter.**

ACTIVITY 4-3

Assigning a Second Resource to Tasks

Data Files:

My Training Manual.mpp

Before You Begin:

The My Training Manual.mpp file is open.

Scenario:

You neglected to consider that you, the project manager, will be involved in interviewing the subject matter expert. You would require two full days to complete the task. Also, it was decided that both you and the writer resource have to work on this task together. Apart from this, you would also like to reduce the duration of Task 4, **Search the Web,** by one day and decide to take the help of another resource.

What You Do	How You Do It
1. Assign **Project Manager 1** as a second resource to Task 5.	a. In the task **Entry** table, in the fifth row, select Task 5, **Interview Subject Matter Experts.**
	b. Scroll to the right and observe that in the **Gantt Chart** view, the **Duration** of the task is **2 days,** and in the **Task Form** view, the **Writer 1** resource is working 100% as displayed in the **Units** column and works for 16 hours as displayed in the **Work** column.
	c. In the task **Entry** table, in the fifth row, in the **Resource Names** column, select **Writer 1.**
	d. In the **Resource Names** column, click after **1,** insert a comma, then type *Project Manager 1* and press **Enter.**

Because additional resources have been assigned to this task, Project recalculates the duration to 1 day, assumes both resources are working 100 percent of their time on this task, and splits the work hours between the two resources as 8 hours each.

2. View the new duration, units, and work values for Task 5.	a. In the task **Entry** table, select Task 5.
	b. Notice that in the **Gantt Chart** view, the duration of the task is reduced to one day, and in the **Task Form** view, both the **Writer 1** and **Project Manager 1** resources are working at 100% and they both work for 8 hours each as displayed in the **Work** column.
	c. On the **Standard** toolbar, click the **Undo** button to remove the **Project Manager 1** resource assigned to task 5.
3. Assign **Project Manager 1** as a second resource, without changing the duration of the task.	a. In the **Task Form** view, uncheck the **Effort driven** check box in order to keep the task's duration constant, independent of the number of assigned resources.
	b. In the **Task Form** view, in the second row, from the **Resource Name** drop-down list, scroll down and select **Project Manager 1.**
	c. In the **Task Form** view, click **OK.**
	d. If necessary, in the **Gantt Chart** view, widen the **Resource Names** column.
	e. Observe that the duration of Task 5 remains the same, at **2 days.** Also, both **Writer 1** and **Project Manager 1** will work for 16 hours.

4. Add **Staff Assistant 1** as a second resource to Task 4.

a. In the task **Entry** view, select Task 4, **Search the Web.**

b. On the **Standard** toolbar, click the **Assign Resources** button to display the **Assign Resources** dialog box.

c. Assign **Staff Assistant 1** to Task 4, **Search the Web.**

d. In the **Assign Resources** dialog box, click **Close.**

e. Drag the divide bar approximately 3 inches to the left to view the **Gantt Chart.**

f. In the **Gantt Chart** view, observe that for Task 4, both **Writer 1** and **Staff Assistant 1** resources are assigned.

g. Save the file.

PRACTICE ACTIVITY 4-4

Assigning Additional Resources

Activity Time: 10 minutes

Data Files:

Task Type.mpp

Before You Begin:

From the C:\084774Data\Managing Resources folder, open the Task Type.mpp file in a combination view with the Gantt Chart's task **Entry** table in the top pane.

Scenario:

Having reviewed the various task types and whether a task is effort-driven or not, you find yourself a bit confused. A colleague has provided you with a sample file that she believes will help clarify these distinctions. You need to work on reducing the task duration by splitting each task between multiple resources.

 Five tasks with the same name, duration, and assigned resources are listed. The task type that has been applied to the task, and whether the **Effort driven** check box is checked or not, is included in parentheses after the task name.

1. Select each task and determine the task type and whether it is effort driven or not.

2. Assign **Writer 2** as a second resource to Task 1. Observe the changes to duration, units, and work.

3. Assign additional resources for each task in the sample file.

4. Save the file as **My Task Type.mpp** and close the file.

TOPIC D
Enter Costs for Resources

You assigned resources to the various tasks. After assigning the resources, you need to estimate the overall cost of the project and each of the resources. In this topic, you will enter the various costs for resources.

Once the resources are assigned to their designated tasks, you may have the need to estimate the overall cost of the project. The total project cost cannot be estimated unless the cost details for individual resources are recorded. With the necessary information entered in the project plan, it would be easy to calculate the total project cost and also identify the resources and tasks that involve huge costs.

How to Enter Costs for Resources

Procedure Reference: Enter Costs for Work and Material Resources using the Resource Sheet

To enter costs for work and material resources using the **Resource Sheet:**

1. Display the **Resource Sheet** view.
2. In the **Resource Name** column, select the desired resource.

 If the resource for which you would like to enter cost is not available, enter it as a new resource.

3. In the desired resource's row, in the **Std. Rate** field, type the cost associated with the resource.
4. If necessary, in the desired resource's row, in the **Ovt. Rate** field, type the overtime cost for the resource.

Procedure Reference: Enter Costs for Work and Material Resources using the Resource Information Dialog Box

To enter costs for work and material resources using the **Resource Information** dialog box:

1. Display the **Resource Sheet** view.
2. Display the **Resource Information** dialog box.
3. Select the **Costs** tab.
4. In the **Cost rate tables** section, on the **A (Default)** tab, in the desired row, in the **Standard Rate** field, type the cost associated with the resource.
5. If necessary, in the desired row, in the **Overtime Rate** field, type the overtime rate of the resource.
6. If there is any change in the cost of the resources, enter the new change.
    *   For a work resource, if the cost change comes into effect on another date, in the desired row, in the **Effective Date** field, enter the new date.
    *   For a material resource, if the rate has increased by some value or percentage, in the next row, in the **Standard Rate** field, enter the value or percentage change.
7. Click **OK**.

Procedure Reference: Enter Costs for a Cost Resource

To enter costs for a cost resource:

1. Display the **Resource Sheet** view.

2. Enter the resource details and from the **Type** drop-down list, select **Cost.**

3. Display the **Gantt Chart** view.

4. Assign the cost resource to the desired task.

5. Display the **Task Usage** view.

6. Select the cost resource assigned to the desired task.

7. Display the **Assignment Information** dialog box.

   ● From the menu, choose **Project→Assignment Information.**

   ● Or, on the **Standard** toolbar, click the **Assignment Information** button.

8. On the **General** tab, in the **Cost** text box, enter the cost for the resource.

9. Click **OK.**

10. If necessary, display the **Gantt Chart** view and widen the **Resource Names** column to view the amount entered for the cost resource.

 A single cost resource that is assigned to different tasks can have different cost values, for example, airfare.

ACTIVITY 4-5

Entering Costs for Resources

Data Files:

My Training Manual.mpp

Before You Begin:

1. The My Training Manual.mpp file is open.
2. From the menu, choose **Window→Remove Split.**
3. From the menu, choose **View→Resource Sheet.**

Scenario:

After assigning the resources to the tasks in your project plan, you now want to update the project plan with the prices related to the resources.

What You Do	How You Do It
1. Enter the cost information for the work resources.	a. In the **Resource Sheet** view, in the 6th row, select the **Std. Rate** field of the **Account Rep 1** resource.
	b. Type **20/hr** and press **Enter.**
	c. In the **Resource Sheet** view, enter the following information:
	• **Writer 1**- *$45/hr*
	• **Editor 1**- *$20/hr*
	• **Artist 1**- *$25/hr*
	• **Subject Matter Expert**- *$100/hr*
	• **Staff Assistant 1**- *$15/hr*
	• **Project Manager 1**- *$60/hr*
	• **Publisher**- *$100,000/yr*
	d. If necessary, double-click the **Std. Rate** column to view the cost.
2. Enter the costs for the material resources.	a. In the **Resource Sheet** view, in the 12th row, in the **Std. Rate** field of the **Glossy Paper** resource, type **10** and press **Enter.**
	b. Enter the costs for the remaining material resources: **$7.50** for **Plain Paper** and **$500** for the **Printer 1** resources.

3. Enter the cost payable to the cost resource.

a. Display the **Gantt Chart** view.

b. If necessary, drag the divide bar to the far right of the application window. Also, widen the **Resource Names** column to display all the names properly.

c. In the 8th row, in Task 8, **Present to Publisher,** select the **Resource Names** field.

d. Click after the closing square bracket, insert a comma, then type *Travel Expenses* and press **Enter.**

e. If necessary, widen the **Resource Names** column.

f. From the menu, choose **View→Task Usage** to display the **Task Usage** view.

g. If necessary, widen the **Task Name** column.

h. In the **Task Name** column, below the **Present to Publisher** task, double-click the **Travel Expenses** resource to display the **Assignment Information** dialog box.

i. On the **General** tab, in the **Cost** text box, triple-click, type *250* and click **OK.**

j. Navigate to the **Gantt Chart** view and widen the **Resource Names** column to view the value entered for the **Travel Expenses** cost resource.

k. Save the file.

TOPIC E
Enter Values for Budget Resources

You entered costs for the resources. Due to management decisions, there may be a cash constraint for your project. In this topic, you will enter values for budget resources.

There may be situations wherein you need to account for the money spent on your resources and tasks. Also, there may be instances when the management impose cash restrictions on a particular project. As a project manager, you need to account for this change in your project plan, so that you do not unnecessarily overshoot the project's cash estimation.

How to Enter Values for Budget Resources

Procedure Reference: Enter Values for Budget Resources

To enter values for budget resources:

1. In the **Resource Sheet** view, enter the budget resource.
2. Display the **Gantt Chart** view.
3. If necessary, display the project summary task.
4. In the project summary task, in the **Resource Names** column, assign the budget resource.
5. From the menu, choose **View→Resource Usage.**
6. In the **Resource Usage** view, insert the **Budget Cost** and **Budget Work** columns.
    a. Choose **Insert→Column** to display the **Column Definition** dialog box.
    b. From the **Field name** drop-down list, select either **Budget Cost** or **Budget Work.**
    c. If necessary, in the **Title** text box, enter a different title.
    d. If necessary, click **Best Fit** to fit the column within the view.
    e. Click **OK.**
7. Insert a **Budget Cost** or a **Budget Work** column depending on your earlier choice.
8. In the type of budget resource column, in the project summary task available below the budget resource, enter the desired budget value.

ACTIVITY 4-6

Entering Values for Budget Resources

Data Files:

My Training Manual.mpp

Before You Begin:

1. The My Training Manual.mpp file is open.

2. Drag the divide bar to the right so that all the columns in the **Gantt Chart** view are displayed.

3. In the **Gantt Chart** view, hide the Indicators and the **Predecessors** columns.

Scenario:

The company management has brought down the overall amount being spent on certain projects. As this move will considerably affect your project, you would like to enter the values estimated for the project in your project plan.

What You Do	How You Do It
1. Assign a budget resource to the project summary task.	a. In the **Gantt Chart,** in the row numbered 0, **My Training Manual,** select the **Resource Names** column.
	b. From the **Resource Names** drop-down list, select **Budget - Miscellaneous** and press **Enter.**
	c. Similarly, assign **Budget - Labor** and **Budget - Material** to the project summary task.
	d. If necessary, widen the **Resource Names** column to view all the budget resources added to the project summary task.

2. In the **Resource Usage** view, add the **Budget Cost** and **Budget Work** columns.

a. From the menu, choose **View→Resource Usage.**

b. If necessary, drag the divide bar to the right to view the **Resource Name** column.

c. In the **Resource Usage** view, from the menu, choose **Insert→Column** to display the **Column Definition** dialog box.

d. In the **Field name** drop-down list, scroll up, select **Budget Cost,** and click **OK** to display the **Budget Cost** column.

e. If necessary, drag the divide bar to the right to view the **Resource Name** column.

f. From the menu, choose **Insert→Column.**

g. In the **Column Definition** dialog box, in the **Field name** drop-down list, scroll up, select **Budget Work** and click **OK** to display the **Budget Work** column.

3. Enter the budgeted values for the budget resources.

a. Drag the divide bar to the right to display all the columns. Also, widen the **Resource Name** column to view all the names.

b. In the **Resource Usage** view, scroll down to view the **Budget - Miscellaneous** resource name.

c. In the row below the **Budget - Miscellaneous** resource, select the **Budget Cost** column for the **My Training Manual** project summary task.

d. Type *1,000* and press **Enter.**

e. In the **My Training Manual** project summary tasks assigned to the **Budget - Labor** and **Budget - Material** resources, in the **Budget Work** column, enter *575 hrs* and *5 reams* respectively.

f. Save and close the file.

TOPIC F
Resolve Resource Conflicts

You entered costs for the resources available in the project plan. Once resources are assigned, you might find that some of the resources are over-scheduled and conflicts exist between the available resources and the tasks. In this topic, you will resolve resource conflicts.

For your project tasks to be accomplished, the assigned resources must perform the necessary work. If the assigned resources are over-scheduled, for example they are working beyond their normal 40-hour work week or are scheduled to work on tasks simultaneously, they may become overwhelmed and be unable to do a good job, thereby putting the success of the project at risk. As a project manager, you might use creative solutions such as reassigning resources, hiring additional resources, requiring overtime work, or perhaps deciding to start the project earlier. How you decide to resolve the issue of overallocations will depend on factors such as cost, resource availability, and schedule flexibility.

Resource Allocation

When planning a project, you might find that conflicts exist between the available resources and the tasks. A resource is *overallocated* when it is scheduled to work beyond its capacity. Overallocations can occur either because a resource is assigned to too many tasks or because more resource units are assigned to a single task.

Resource Allocation Views

Project offers several views for displaying the resource allocation information. Within these views, overallocations are identified in various ways, depending on the view that you are looking at.

 The various options on the **Resource Management** toolbar assist you in managing the resources of your project.

Examples of Resource Allocation in Various Views

In the **Resource Sheet** view, the allocated resources appear as red and are indicated by an exclamation point in the **Indicators** column. In the **Resource Graph** view, they appear as a red bar. In the **Resource Usage** view, the overallocated resource name is red and the units will appear as over 100-percent allocated.

Leveling

Once you have identified any overallocated resources in a project plan, you will need to determine the way in which you can level out the tasks for these resources. Microsoft Project offers a possible solution called *leveling*. Leveling is the process of delaying or splitting tasks to resolve conflicts. Tasks are either split or delayed until the resources assigned are no longer overloaded. As a result, leveling can extend the project's finish date. It is important to note that leveling does not change resource assignments, nor does it add additional resources. By default, resources are not leveled automatically. By manually leveling overallocated resources, you can make leveling decisions based on other project factors such as lowest cost, earliest project finish date, or resource schedules.

Slack

When Project levels your overallocated resources, it determines the tasks that have to be split or delayed by looking at the task ID, available slack, task priority, task dependencies, task constraints, and scheduling dates. Slack is the amount of time a task can slip before it affects another task's dates or the project finish date.

The Resource Leveling Options

The different sections in the **Resource Leveling** dialog box have options that help you in leveling the overallocated resources.

Section Name	Description
Leveling calculations	Allows you to specify whether the resources should be leveled automatically or manually upon the detection of an overallocated resource. Also, you can select a time period for the project; based on this time period, you can determine whether there are any overallocated resources.
Leveling range	Allows you to choose an option based on which you can level the entire project or only those tasks falling under the specified time period.
Resolving overallocations	Allows you to specify the order in which the overallocated tasks can be delayed or split. It also allows you to level the task within the available slack period, and create a split within the remaining tasks and assignments.

How to Resolve Resource Conflicts

Procedure Reference: Resolve Resource Conflicts Using Manual Leveling

To resolve resource conflicts using manual leveling:

1. From the menu, choose **Tools→Level Resources** to display the **Resource Leveling** dialog box.

 Before leveling, please save the file with a different name, so that you have a copy of the earlier version of the project plan in case you are not pleased with the leveling results.

2. In the **Leveling calculations** section, verify that the **Manual** option is selected.

3. In the **Leveling range for (heading)** section, select the desired option for leveling the project:

   - Select **Level entire project** to level the entire project plan.

   - Select **Level** and include a **From** and **To** range of dates to level a portion of your project plan.

4. In the **Resolving overallocations** section, select a leveling order to determine the task that is to be delayed or split in order to resolve resource overallocations. The default leveling order is **Standard.**

5. In the **Resolving overallocations** section, check the desired check box for leveling.

   - Check the **Level only within available slack** check box, if you do not want Project to delay your project finish date (off by default). If you check this setting, you may still have overallocations in your project after leveling.

   - Check the **Leveling can adjust individual assignments on a task** check box, if you want Project to level a resource independent of other resources working on the same task (on by default).

   - Check the **Leveling can create splits in remaining work** check box, if you want Project to interrupt tasks by creating splits in the remaining work on tasks or resource assignments (on by default).

   - Check the **Level resources with the proposed booking type** check box, if you want Project to include tasks using proposed and confirmed resources.

6. Click **Level Now.**

7. If necessary, in the **Level Now** dialog box, click **OK** to use the entire resource pool.

8. Review the changes in the **Leveling Gantt Chart** view; and if you are pleased with the results, save the file.

The Leveling Gantt Chart

The **Leveling Gantt Chart** allows you to see the results of leveling. The original schedule is depicted by green bars, and the gap between a task's green and blue bars represents the delay added due to the leveling process.

View Overallocated Resources

You can view the overallocated resources by choosing **Project→Filtered for:→Overallocated Resources.** In the **Resource Graph** view, if the resource is overallocated, it would be displayed in red and in the bar chart, red bars indicate that the resource has exceeded the maximum unit and working time that are available in the given time period. To view the full list of resources, choose **Project→Filtered for:→All Resources.** You can also view the overallocated resources in the **Resource Usage** or the **Resource Sheet** views as their names would be displayed in red with an **Indicator,** ◇ symbol appearing beside it.

ACTIVITY 4-7

Resolving Resource Conflicts

Data Files:

Training Manual Allocations.mpp

Before You Begin:

1. From the C:\084774Data\Managing Resources folder, open the Training Manual Allocations.mpp file.

2. Display the **Resource Sheet** view.

Scenario:

Your colleague assigned all the remaining resources to the tasks in the project plan. You would like to view the data to ensure that the resources have been assigned tasks correctly and they are not burdened with too many tasks. If any resource is assigned with many tasks, you would like to reduce their tasks.

What You Do	How You Do It
1. Which resources are overallocated?	
2. Display the resource graph information for **Writer 1** for the weeks between July 30, 2007 and August 6, 2007.	a. Display the **Resource Graph** view.
	b. Right-click the **Standard** toolbar, and choose **Resource Management** to display the **Resource Management** toolbar.
	c. In the right side of the graph, scroll to display the weeks between July 30, 2007 and August 6, 2007.
	d. In the **Resource Graph** view, observe that the blue bars indicate that the **Writer 1** resource is working at 100 percent while the red bars indicate that the resource is overallocated on several days in August.

3. Display the resources in the **Resource Usage** view.

    a. Right-click the active pane indicator and choose **Resource Usage.**

    b. In the **Resource Usage** view, observe that the **Writer 1** and **Editor 1** resources are overallocated.

 If another resource is displayed, use the horizontal scroll bar as necessary.

    c. In the **Resource Usage** view, scroll down to view the **Staff Assistant 2** resource to be overallocated.

4. Display the project finish date.

    a. From the menu, choose **Project→Project Information** to display the **Project Information for 'Training Manual Allocations.mpp'** dialog box.

    b. In the **Finish date** text box, observe that **Wed 10/10/07** is displayed and click **OK** to close the dialog box.

5. Strike a balance in tasks for the overallocated resources.

    a. Save the file as ***My Training Manual Allocations.mpp*** to preserve a copy of the file prior to leveling.

    b. From the menu, choose **Tools→Level Resources.**

    c. In the **Leveling calculations** section, observe that the **Manual** option is selected and click **Level Now.**

    d. In the **Level Now** dialog box, click **OK.**

 Do not use **Automatic** leveling because this will allow Project to level any overallocated resource immediately, preventing you from choosing to level or not to level.

e. From the menu, choose **View→More Views.**

f. In the **More Views** dialog box, in the **Views** list box, scroll up and select **Leveling Gantt.**

g. Click **Apply.**

h. In the **Leveling Gantt** view, on the right side, scroll to display the weeks between July 30, 2007 and August 6, 2007.

i. In the **Leveling Gantt** view, place the mouse pointer over the green bar for Task 5, **Interview Subject Matter Experts.** Observe that the screentip displays the preleveled start and finish time along with the duration for the task.

```
                    Preleveled Task
Task: Interview Subject Matter Experts
Preleveled Start: Thu 08/09/07    Duration: 2.04d
Preleveled Finish: Fri 08/10/07
```

j. Place the mouse pointer over the blue bar for Task 4, **Search the Web.** Observe that the screentip displays the actual start and finish dates along with its duration.

```
                    Task
Task: Search the Web
Start: Thu 08/02/07    Duration: 8d
Finish: Mon 08/13/07
```

k. Save and close the file.

Lesson 4 Follow-up

In this lesson, you managed the resources in your project plan. Managing resources will enable you to keep track of the total work done and the resources used for completing the project.

1. **Will you need to create any resource calendars for your project plans?**

2. **How will understanding the relationship between task work, task duration, and task units help you when assigning multiple resources to a single task?**

5 Finalizing the Project Plan

Lesson Time: 1 hour(s)

Lesson Objectives:

In this lesson, you will finalize the project plan.

You will:

- Display the project plan's critical path.
- Shorten the project duration.
- Set a project baseline.
- Print a project summary report.

Introduction

You have a project plan that includes task and assigned resources. With this data entered into the project plan, Project calculates a project finish date. Because this finish date may not always be acceptable, you need to identify some techniques for shortening the total project duration, as well as capturing project plan information for future comparison. In this lesson, you will finalize the project plan.

Although Project will calculate a project finish date, as a project manager, you will need to determine whether this project finish date is acceptable or not. In many cases, you will have to change task parameters so that the project finishes earlier. To be able to control the schedule using Project, you must be familiar with techniques for shortening the total project duration, as well as, ways to preserve the original project plan data.

TOPIC A
Display the Critical Path

Now that you have a complete list of tasks with resources assigned, you are ready to finalize your project. At this point, you will want to check your project finish date to determine whether it is acceptable. As a result, you may find that the schedule needs to be adjusted. To adjust the total project duration using Project, you will need to identify those project tasks that affect the project end date. In this topic, you will display the project's critical path.

As a project manager, you will need to reduce a project's total duration at some point or the other. The idea is to get the job done in an acceptable time frame, within an agreed-upon budget, and meet the project specifications. To reduce the total duration, you will need to know which tasks in the project plan actually affect the project's finish date. Your job, as a project manager, will include paying close attention to managing these tasks.

Critical Path

Definition:

A *critical path* is the series of tasks that determines the calculated finish date of the project. If a non-critical series of linked tasks slips its dates, this series of tasks will become the critical path. In a project, the critical path can show if the project will finish on time and also highlight the danger points. Tasks on the critical path are called *critical tasks*, if one or more of these critical tasks are delayed, the project will finish late. In complex or large projects, there can be more than one critical path or critical path section and the critical path can change many times throughout a project's life cycle.

Example:

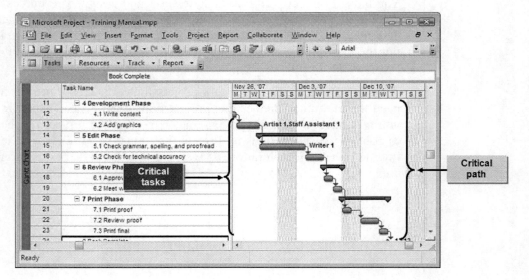

The Gantt Chart Wizard

The **Gantt Chart Wizard** has options that allow you to customize your **Gantt Chart.** The wizard can be used to display the critical path in the **Gantt Chart** view. The wizard has options to configure bar styles and lay out options. Running the **Gantt Chart Wizard** reconfigures any manually applied bar styles.

The Bar Styles Dialog Box

The **Bar Styles** dialog box is used to format the **Gantt Chart** bars. It is used to emphasize attributes including; critical tasks, milestones, summary tasks, and slacks. One set of style is associated with each chart-type view.

How to Display a Critical Path

Procedure Reference: Display the Critical Path

To view the critical path:

1. From the menu, choose **Format→Gantt Chart Wizard.**

2. In the **Gantt Chart Wizard,** click **Next** to go to the next page.

3. On the second page of the wizard, verify that the **Critical path** option is selected and click **Next** to specify that the critical tasks in the **Gantt Chart** should be highlighted and to move to the next page.

4. On the third page of the wizard, verify that the **Resources and dates** option is selected and click **Next** to specify that the resources and the dates in the Gantt bars should be displayed and to move to the next page.

5. On the fourth page of the wizard, verify that the **Yes** option is selected and click **Next** to specify that the link must be shown between dependent tasks and to move to the next page.

6. Click **Format It** to apply the custom **Gantt Chart.**

7. Click **Exit Wizard** to view the newly formatted **Gantt Chart.**

8. If necessary, choose **View→Network Diagram** to view the critical path in a diagram view.

ACTIVITY 5-1

Displaying the Critical Path

Data Files:

Training Manual.mpp

Before You Begin:

From the C:\084774Data\Finalizing the Project folder, open the Training Manual mpp file.

Scenario:

Your have called for a status meeting, wherein you need to highlight the problem areas in the project. You need to identify the tasks that need attention in your project to finish the project as scheduled as it is nearing the target finish date. You also want to view the tasks like a flow chart.

What You Do	How You Do It
1. Display the critical path in the **Gantt Chart** wizard.	a. Choose **Format→Gantt Chart Wizard**.
	b. In the **Gantt Chart Wizard**, click **Next** to move to the next page.
	c. Select the **Critical path** option and click **Next** to highlight the critical tasks in the **Gantt Chart** and move to the next page.
	d. Verify that the **Resources and dates** option is selected and click **Next** to specify the resources and the dates in the Gantt bars and move to the next page.
	e. Verify that the **Yes** option is selected and click **Next** to show the link among the dependent tasks.
	f. Click **Format It** to apply the custom **Gantt Chart**.
	g. Click **Exit Wizard** to close the wizard and to view the critical tasks.
	h. In the **Gantt Chart**, scroll to the right to view changes.
	i. Observe that the critical tasks are represented by red bars and non-critical tasks are represented by blue bars in the **Gantt Chart**.

2. Display the critical path in a **Network Diagram.**

    a.   From the menu, choose **View→Network Diagram.**

    b.   Observe that the critical tasks are represented by red bars and non-critical tasks are represented by blue bars in the **Network Diagram.**

    c.   Save the file as *My Training Manual.mpp*

TOPIC B
Shorten the Project Duration

With the critical tasks identified, you now know the tasks that you have to work with to shorten the total project duration. You need to identify the various techniques for modifying the project end date. In this topic, you will shorten the project duration.

Knowing how to shorten the total project duration is key to being a successful project manager. As project manager, you will have to make decisions that may include assigning additional resources to tasks on the critical path, dividing tasks, or removing project requirements to shorten the total project duration.

Slack

Slack is the amount of time that a task can slip before it affects another task or the project's finish date. **Free Slack** is the amount of time a task can slip before it delays another task. **Total Slack** is the amount of time a task can slip before it delays the project finish date. If **Total Slack** is a negative number, it indicates the amount of time that must be saved so that the project finish date is not extended. Slack is displayed by the **Detail Gantt** view and is represented by thin green bars that extend from a Gantt bar for a task.

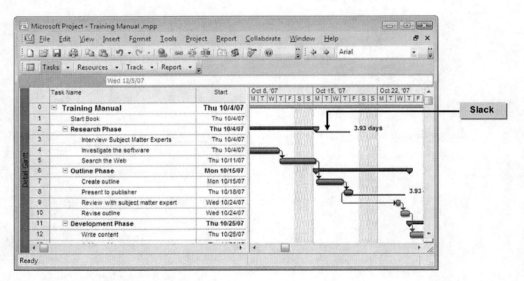

Figure 5-1: *Project with slack displayed.*

How to Shorten the Project Duration

Procedure Reference: Assign Additional Resources to a Task on the Critical Path

To assign additional resources to a task on the critical path:

1. Use the **Gantt Chart Wizard** to display the critical path in the **Gantt Chart** view.
2. Select a critical task that you wish to add additional resources to.
3. On the **Standard** toolbar, click the **Assign Resources** button.
4. In the **Assign Resources** dialog box, select the resources to be added to the critical task.
5. Click **Assign** and then click **Close** to assign the additional resource.

Procedure Reference: Divide Tasks

To divide tasks:

1. From the **Task Name**, select a task to be divided into two tasks.
2. Select the text of the task and type the desired task name and press the **Enter** key.
3. In the **Duration** column, type the desired duration and press the **Enter** key.
4. Insert a task row above the divided task to add another task.
5. Type the task name and duration for this newly created task.
6. If necessary, assign another resource to the divided task.

Removing a Task

To remove a task from the project plan, select the row indicator for the task to be deleted and press **Delete** to remove the task.

Procedure Reference: Identify Slack in the Project Plan

To identify slack in a project plan:

1. From the menu, choose **View→More Views.**
2. In the **More Views** dialog box, select **Detail Gantt** and click **Apply.**
3. From the menu, choose **View→Table:Schedule→Schedule.**
4. In the **Gantt Chart**, slack appears as thin green bars to the right of the tasks, with slack values adjoining the Gantt bars.
5. If necessary, on the **Standard** toolbar, click the **Scroll to Task** button to view the Gantt bar for the task.

ACTIVITY 5-2

Assigning Additional Resources to a Task on the Critical Path

Data Files:

My Training Manual.mpp

Before You Begin:

The My Training Manual.mpp file is open.

Scenario:

Based on the requirements, you know that the current project finish date is unacceptable and needs to be moved up by several days. As you need to move up the finish date, you need to identify tasks that are getting delayed. You know that Task 16, would need another editor to complete the task on time. You decide to take the help of another editor and include this in the project plan.

What You Do	How You Do It
1. Display the **Detail Gantt,** to view the slack time.	a. In the **Network Diagram** view, choose **View→More Views.**
	b. In the **More Views** dialog box, in the **Views** list box, double-click **Detail Gantt.**
	c. Place the mouse pointer over the 2nd green line that extends from the Gantt bar for Task 2, to view the screentip for slack time.
2. Display the Gantt bar for the selected task.	a. Observe the current project finish date.
	b. Display the **Gantt Chart** view.
	c. In the **Gantt Chart** view, in the **Task Name** column, select Task 16.
	d. On the **Standard** toolbar, click the **Scroll to Task** button to view the Gantt bar for the task.

3. Add **Editor 2** as a second resource to Task 16.

   a. If necessary, in the **Gantt Chart** view, scroll to the right and drag the divide bar to the right so that all the columns are visible.

   b. In the **Resource Names** column, in the drop-down list for Task 16, type a comma (,) and select **Editor 2** and press **Enter.**

   c. Observe that the project finishes earlier and the project finish date has moved up by a single day.

   d. Save the file.

4. **Why aren't we adding more resources to non-critical tasks?**

ACTIVITY 5-3
Dividing Tasks

Data Files:

My Training Manual.mpp

Before You Begin:

The My Training Manual.mpp file is open.

Scenario:

You need to move up the project finish date. So you negotiate for an additional writer to be added to the project team. With the additional writer, you decide that Writer 1 will work on lessons 1 through 5 and Writer 2 on lessons 6 through 10. These tasks need be done simultaneously and these changes need to be reflected in the project plan.

What You Do	How You Do It
1. Divide Task 12 into two separate tasks.	a. Select Task 12.
	b. In the **Task Name** column, select the text and type ***Write Lessons 1-5*** and press **Enter.**
	c. In the **Gantt Chart** view, in the **Duration** column for Task 12, type ***12.5*** and press **Enter.**

 The work breakdown numbers are automatically edited.

d. Select Task 13 and press the **Insert** key to insert a new task above Task 13.

e. Type the task name as ***Write Lessons 6-10*** and enter the duration as ***12.5.***

2. Remove **Writer 2** from Task 12 and assign it to Task 13.

    a. Select Task 12.

    b. Click and drag the divide bar to the right to view all the columns in the **Gantt Chart.**

    c. On the **Standard** toolbar, click the **Assign Resources** button to display the **Assign Resources** dialog box.

    d. In the **Resources from My Training Manual.mpp** section, select the **Writer 2** resource.

    e. Click **Remove** to remove the second resource assigned to task **Write Lessons 1-5.**

    f. In the **Assign Resources** dialog box, click **Close.**

    g. Select Task 13, **Write Lessons 6-10** and assign **Writer 2.**

    h. Observe that the project finish date remains the same in spite of adding an additional resource.

3. **Why hasn't the project finish date changed to reflect the task division?**

4. Change the task relationship type so that both tasks occur simultaneously.

    a. In the task **Entry** table, select the **Predecessors** field for Task 13, **Write Lessons 6–10.**

    b. In row 13, in the **Predecessors** field for Task 13, click after the number **12,** type *SS* and press **Enter.**

    c. Observe that the project finish date has moved up after changing the task relationship.

    d. Save the file.

ACTIVITY 5-4
Removing Project Requirements

Data Files:

My Training Manual.mpp

Before You Begin:

The My Training Manual.mpp file is open.

Scenario:

You have heard from your client that the software is going to be shipped without the feature that was to be presented in Appendix A of the training manual. Because this Appendix is no longer needed, you decide to update the project plan.

What You Do	How You Do It
1. Delete Task 14.	a. Select the ID number for Task 14.
	b. Press **Delete.**
	c. Click anywhere in the **Gantt Chart.**
2. View the project finish date.	a. Observe that the project finish date has changed, indicating that the project finish date has moved up.
	b. Save the file.

TOPIC C
Set a Baseline

You entered tasks, task durations, resources, resource assignments, cost data, and made necessary adjustments to the schedule. You can now consider your project plan to be finalized. However, before you begin tracking progress on the project, you will want to preserve your original project estimates so that you will have some data to compare the actual project results with. In this topic, you will set a project baseline.

Once your project begins, you will enter information about how things are actually happening, and the current information will be altered. As you plan to calculate variances between the original plan and the actual project progress for project variables such as task duration, start and finish dates, or costs, saving a project baseline is essential. Setting a baseline creates a benchmark for future reference, and this can then be observed within the project file.

Baselines

Baselines are original project plans used to monitor a project's progress. It includes tasks, resources, assignments, and cost estimates. After you enter the complete project information in your project plan, you save a baseline plan, so that you can view the results in the task sheet view. The dates in the start and finish fields are copied to the baseline start and baseline finish fields, and so on for several fields. In effect, this saves a copy of the current date information for future reference.

The Set Baseline Dialog Box

The **Set Baseline** dialog box is used to set a baseline plan or interim plan for tasks, resources, and assignments, for the entire project, or selected tasks. You can set up to 11 different baselines. The start and finish dates for tasks are updated as you adjust and track your project using baselines.

The Project Statistics Dialog Box

The **Project Statistics** dialog box is used to review the scheduled timing and sequence of tasks within a project against the actual information that shows what has actually occurred. It shows the variance between the saved baseline plan and the current schedule of the start and finish dates, durations, work, and costs. It is accessed from the **Project Information** dialog box.

How to Set a Baseline

Procedure Reference: Set a Baseline Plan

To set a baseline plan:

1. On the **Standard** toolbar, choose **Tools→Tracking→Set Baseline.**
2. In the **Set Baseline** dialog box, check **Set baseline** to set the baseline plan.
3. In the **For** section, select the **Entire project** or **Selected tasks** option to set the baseline plan as needed.
4. Click **OK** to set the baseline.

Procedure Reference: Clear a Baseline Plan

To clear a baseline plan:

1. On the **Standard** toolbar, choose **Tools→Tracking→Clear Baseline.**
2. In the **Clear Baseline** dialog box, select the desired option to clear the baseline plan.
3. In the **For** section, select the desired option to clear the baseline plan as needed.
4. Click **OK** to clear the baseline.

Project Statistics

Once you set the baseline plan, the baseline statistics are displayed in the **Project Statistics** dialog box, which is accessed by choosing **Project→Project information,** and then clicking **Statistics** in the **Project Information** dialog box. The presence of baseline statistics generates variance statistics and displays them in the dialog box. Project calculates the variance statistics by subtracting the baseline statistics from the current statistic. For example, start variance is the difference between the planned start and the scheduled start.

ACTIVITY 5-5

Setting a Baseline Plan

Data Files:

My Training Manual.mpp

Before You Begin:

The My Training Manual.mpp file is open.

Scenario:

As a project manager, before the project work begins, you want to capture your original project estimates so that you can later compare them to actual project results to see how you are progressing as against the plan.

What You Do	How You Do It
1. Display the **Project Statistics** dialog box.	a. From the menu, choose **Project→Project Information**.
	b. In the **Project Information for 'My Training Manual.mpp'** dialog box, click **Statistics**.
	c. Observe that the **Baseline** row in the **Start** and **Finish** columns read **NA** indicating that a baseline has not yet been set.
	d. Click **Close**.

2. Set a baseline plan and display the **Project Statistics** dialog box.

    a. From the menu, choose **Tools→Tracking→Set Baseline.**

    b. In the **Set Baseline** dialog box, verify that the **Set baseline** option is selected and also verify that in the **For** section, the **Entire project** option is selected.

    c. Click **OK** to accept the defaults and set a baseline for the entire project.

    d. Display the **Project Statistics** dialog box.

    e. Observe that the **Baseline** dates match the **Current Start** and **Finish** dates because no work has been done on the project.

    f. Click **Close.**

    g. Save the file.

TOPIC D
Print a Project Summary Report

You finalized your project plan and saved a baseline plan for your project. You may now wish to display, analyze, print, or distribute your project plan data. In this topic, you will print a project summary report.

Having your project plan on your computer's hard drive as a .mpp file will be extremely helpful to you. However, it would not help during discussions with team members, for instance, to have a group of people at a project status meeting crowd around your laptop, to view your project's cost data. You would rather print a view with a cost table applied or generate a cost report to distribute to the group. Project offers a variety of built-in views and reports that can help you print and analyze project data.

Reports

Definition:

A *report* is a format for generating project information that is appropriate for distribution. Basic reports are divided into six categories. You can change any of these reports to present the information that you want. If none of the default reports meet your information needs, you can use a template to create a custom basic report.

 Microsoft Office Project 2007 includes custom visual reports, which provide rich reporting options that can be used in Microsoft Office Excel and Microsoft Office Visio.

Example:

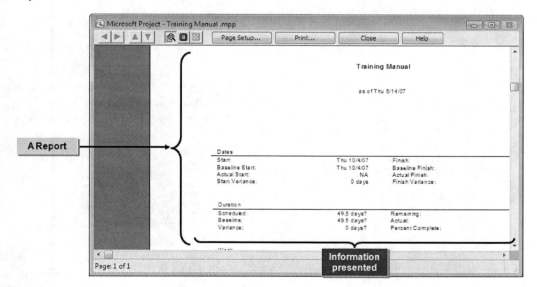

Report Types

The six different categories of reports in Project allow you to select the most appropriate format to display your data.

Report Category	Description
Overview	 This category is used to select, edit, and generate a report to summarize the number of tasks, project costs, or to list the critical tasks or working times for each day. There are five standard report types in this category.
Current Activities	 This report category is intended for more frequent usage and geared toward audiences more directly involved with the tasks in the project. There are six standard reports in this category.
Costs	 This is a category that is effective in tracking the budget cost of a project. There are five standard reports for reviewing your project's costs and budget.
Assignments	 This category is used to generate the to-do lists for resources and their assigned tasks, to follow up with resources and their current task progress, or to determine who has too many assignments in the available time. There are four standard reports in this category.

Report Category	Description
Workload	 This category has excellent tracking tools for viewing the amount of work assigned to a task or per resource, on a weekly basis. There are two reports in this category.
Custom	 This report category is used to adapt an existing report or create an entirely new report.

How to Print a Project Summary Report

Procedure Reference: Print a Project Summary Report

To print a project summary report:

1. Choose **Report→Reports.**
2. In the **Reports** dialog box, click the icon of the report category you want to print.
3. Click **Select** to display the dialog box for the selected report category.
4. Click the icon of the report that you want to print.
5. Click **Select** to display the print preview of the report.
6. Click **Print** to print the report.
7. In the **Print** dialog box, click **OK** to print the report.

Print a View

A view is a visual representation of the tasks or resources in a project. Most views can be printed by selecting the view and choosing **File→Print**.

ACTIVITY 5-6

Printing a Project Summary Report

Data Files:

My Training Manual.mpp

Before You Begin:

The My Training Manual.mpp file is open.

Scenario:

As a manager for the training manual project you want to discuss the total cost of your project with your team. You also want to refer to the project summary information such as project start and finish dates, duration, work hours, and costs. You need to quickly refer resource information, specifically who does what tasks when. With the above data you plan to conduct a meeting with your team.

What You Do	How You Do It
1. Display the **Gantt Chart** with the cost table applied.	a. Choose **View→Table: Entry→Cost.**
	b. Widen columns in the **Gantt Chart** as necessary to view all the columns.
	c. Observe the total estimated current project cost.
	d. If necessary, on the **Standard** toolbar, click the **Print** button to print the view.
2. Display the **Overview Reports.**	a. Choose **Report→Reports.**
	b. In the **Reports** dialog box, verify that **Overview** is selected.
	c. Click **Select** to display the **Overview Reports** dialog box, to view the various report types.

3. Preview the **Project Summary** report.

   a. In the **Overview Reports** dialog box, verify that **Project Summary** is selected.

   b. Click **Select** to display the print preview of the report to be printed.

   c. On the toolbar, click the **Zoom** button to get a better look of the report.

   d. Click **Close.**

4. Print the **Who Does What When** report.

   a. In the **Reports** dialog box, display the **Assignments** reports.

   b. Display the preview of the **Who Does What When**, **Assignment Reports**.

   c. In the print preview of the report, on the toolbar, click the **Page Right,** ▶ button to move to the next page.

   d. Zoom to review the page two of the **Who Does What When** report.

   e. In the print preview of the report, on the toolbar, click **Print.**

   f. In the **Print** dialog box, click **OK.**

   g. Close the **Reports** dialog box.

   h. Save the file.

   i. From the menu, choose **File→Exit** to close the Project application.

Lesson 5 Follow-up

In this lesson, you finalized the project plan. The different finalization techniques will help you identify the tasks that may delay your project, shorten your project duration, preserve the original project plan, and share your project data in the desired format.

1. **Give examples of techniques that you have used to shorten a project's total duration?**

2. **Why would you set a baseline for a project plan?**

3. **What project reports are you likely to generate once a project is finalized?**

Follow-up

In this course, you set up a functional project plan using Microsoft® Office Project Professional 2007 software. By creating a project plan, organizing tasks within it, assigning resources, and finalizing the plan, you will be able to effectively manage project information, calculate and maintain the project schedule, track project costs, and analyze and communicate project data.

1. What is the single feature of Project that you will certainly use? Which features will you least likely use?

2. Back at work, what role will you most likely have in future project plans? How can you see your department or company using Project?

3. How might you use Project to help you in assigning resources and costs to your project plans?

What's Next?

Microsoft® Project 2007: Level 2 is the next course in this series.

Lesson Labs

Due to classroom setup constraints, some labs cannot be keyed in sequence immediately following their associated lesson. Your instructor will tell you whether your labs can be practiced immediately following the lesson or whether they require separate setup from the main lesson content.

Lesson 1 Lab 1

Exploring a Project in Various Views

Activity Time: 5 minutes

Objective:

Explore a project in various views.

Data Files:

HTML Training Manual.mpp, XML Training Manual.mpp

Before You Begin:

Launch the Microsoft Project application.

Scenario:

You have recently joined the project management team of an organization. In a week's time, you will be assigned your first project, and your supervisor has given you samples of various project plans. As you are unfamiliar with Microsoft Project 2007, you decide to familiarize yourself with the software and get a feel of how the project tasks and resources are represented in the sample project plans. There are two samples provided to you—HTML Training Manual.mpp and XML Training Manual.mpp.

1. Open the **HTML Training Manual.mpp** file from the **C:\084774Data\Getting Started** folder in the default view.

2. Use screentips to identify any screen elements that you are curious about.

3. Display the view where you will be able to review all tasks and task dependencies in a tabular format.

4. Close the **HTML Training Manual.mpp** file.

5. Open the **XML Training Manual.mpp** file from the **C:\084774Data\Getting Started** folder in the default view.

6. Go to **More Views** using the **View Bar.**

7. Display the **Resource Name Form** to view task entries, schedule, and work information about each resource.

8. Close the **XML Training Manual.mpp** file.

Lesson 2 Lab 1

Creating a New Workspace Project Plan

Activity Time: 10 minutes

Objective:

Create a new project plan for the new workspace project.

Before You Begin:

The Microsoft Project application is open.

Scenario:

Create a new project plan for the new workspace project. You want to use the Project application to manage your project. You have the following general information about your project:

- Subject: Refurbish New Offices
- Manager: *Your Name*
- Company: Our Global Company
- Project start date: September 1, 2007

Also, you would like to summarize your project, and you have identified the various tasks with their durations and the resources involved in the project. The details are as follows:

- Initial Milestone: Project Start
- Paint the Walls - 2 days
- Install Partitions - 1 day
- Install Network Cables - 3 days
- Lay Carpet - 2 days
- Prepare Offices - 5 days
- Assemble Furniture - 2 days
- Hook up Computers - 1 day
- Move in Belongings - 2 days
- Project End - 0 day
- Resources: Laborer, Painters 1 and 2, and Technician

1. Generate a new project plan.

2. Use the **Project Guide** toolbar to enter the project start date as *9/1/2007.*

3. Save the new project file as *My New Workspace.mpp*

4. Enter the project's summary information.

5. Enter the project tasks, milestones, and durations.

6. Display the initial project summary task.

7. If necessary, expand the columns of the view to display the column data.

8. Enter the resource information.

9. Save and close the file.

Lesson 3 Lab 1

Organizing Tasks in a Project Plan

Activity Time: 10 minutes

Objective:

Organize the tasks in the New Workspace project plan.

Data Files:

New Workspace.mpp

Before You Begin:

From the C:\084774Data\Managing Tasks folder, open the New Workspace.mpp file.

Scenario:

You have a project plan, New Workspace.mpp, which includes tasks and durations. You realize that certain tasks can be converted to subtasks to enable viewing the hierarchy of the various tasks. You plan to have a staff meeting for 1 hour every week on Mondays from October 08, 2007 to November 12, 2007. To determine the project time line, you decide to link all milestones and subtasks using the default relationship. You then modify the relationship between similar tasks so that they can start at the same time. You want to park a reminder to check cable wires for the task **Install Network Cables**. You also realize that the painters will be available only on October 08, 2007 to paint the walls. As a project manager, you have to ensure that the project finishes as scheduled; so you set a target date for the completion of the task **Move in Belongings** as October 24, 2007.

1. In the **New Workspace.mpp** file, indent tasks **Assemble Furniture, Hook up Computers** and **Move in Belongings** as subtasks of the task **Prepare Offices.**

2. Display the outline numbers for the newly indented tasks.

3. Link all milestones and subtasks to a finish-to-start relationship.

4. Change the task relationship between the tasks **Install Partitions** and **Install Network Cables** to a start-to-start relationship.

5. Add the weekly recurring task, **Staff Meeting.**

6. Set a constraint for the task **Paint the Walls.**

7. Set a deadline for the task **Move in Belongings.**

8. Add task notes for the task **Install Network Cables.**

9. Save the file as *My New Workspace.mpp*

10. Close the project plan.

Lesson 4 Lab 1

Managing Resources in the New Workspace Project Plan

Activity Time: 10 minutes

Objective:

Manage resources in the new workspace project plan.

Data Files:

New Workspace.mpp

Before You Begin:

From the C:\084774Data\Managing Resources folder, open the New Workspace.mpp file.

Scenario:

As the project manager, for the new workspace project, you have spent most of the month of September purchasing materials, lining up contractors and labor resources, and confirming the delivery dates. Due to some unavoidable reasons, the laborer resource could work only in the afternoons (13:00 to 17:00). You received the cost information for the resources and the tasks these resources would perform. You need to enter this information in your project plan. Also, you want to ensure that none of the resources in the plan are overallocated. The following list provides the details about the tasks performed by the resources and their cost information.

- Task 9: Paint the Walls - Painter 1 resource
- Task 10: Install Partitions - Laborer
- Task 11: Install Network Cables - Technician
- Task 12: Lay Carpet - Laborer
- Task 14: Assemble Furniture - Laborer
- Task 15: Hook up Computers - Technician
- Task 16: Move in Belongings - Laborer
- Laborer charges $50 per hour.
- Technician charges $100 per hour.
- Both the painters charge $65 per hour.

---

1. Create a resource calendar for the laborer resource.

---

2. Assign the resources to their tasks.

---

3. Because the technician needs assistance for fixing the network cables, you need to assign the laborer as a second resource to task 4, **Install Network Cables.**

---

4. Because the painter resource needs assistance for painting the walls, you need to assign another painter resource to task 9, **Paint the Walls.**

5. Enter the cost information for the resources.

6. View the overallocation of the **Laborer** resource in a view of your choice.

7. Save the file as *My New Workspace.mpp*

8. Level the entire resource pool.

9. Save and close the file.

Lesson 5 Lab 1

Finalizing the Project

Activity Time: 10 minutes

Objective:

Finalize the project plan by identifying its critical path, shortening its duration, saving a baseline, and previewing a report.

Data Files:

New Workspace.mpp

Before You Begin:

From the C:\084774Data\Finalizing the Project folder, open the New Workspace.mpp file.

Scenario:

You finished the planning phase of your project plan, New Workspace.mpp. The current end date of November 8, 2007 is unacceptable. You know that the second task cannot be finished within the given time frame with the available resources. So you decide to use another resource to complete a part of the task. You then save the original project plan and preview the **Project Summary** report.

1. View the project finish date.

2. Split Task 9, **Paint the Walls** into the following two tasks:
   - Paint the East Walls, with a 1-day duration, Painter 1
   - Paint the West Walls, with a 1-day duration, Painter 2

3. Change the task relationship between Tasks 10 and 11 to allow for both tasks to occur simultaneously.

4. Determine whether the end date has changed.

5. Save a baseline for the entire project.

6. Preview the **Project Summary** report.

7. Save the file as *My New Workspace.mpp* and close the file.

Solutions

Lesson 1

Activity 1-1

1. **Identify the screen element that helps you create a new project from scratch?**

    a) The Standard toolbar

    ✓ b) The Task pane

    c) The Gantt Chart

    d) The Project Guide toolbar

2. **True or False? During the Monitoring and Controlling phase of project management, the project manager balances the demands of scope, time, and quality; tracks corrective action; and reports progress.**

    ✓ True

    ___ False

Activity 1-2

3. **What is the default view in Project? What table is applied to the default view?**

    The Gantt Chart is the default view, with the task Entry table displayed.

Lesson 2

Activity 2-2

1. **Does the Project Guide toolbar offer any options for working with calendars?**

    Yes, the Tasks side pane offers the Define general working times link.

3. **What is the default project calendar?**

    The Standard calendar is the default project calendar.

4. **What are the defaults for the work week and for the work-day hours?**

   The Standard calendar defaults include a five-day work week, Monday through Friday, with eight-hour days (8:00 a.m.–12:00 p.m. and 1:00 p.m.–5:00 p.m., excluding a 1-hour lunch).

6. **What indication do you receive that these dates have been marked as non-working days?**

   The dates that have been marked as non-working days have a different background color in the calendar. Also, when these dates are selected, the From and To columns of the Details dialog box are empty.

Activity 2-3

2. **What are the screen changes that have occurred as a result of entering the Start Book task?**

   The following changes have occurred: The task has been entered and is assigned an ID number of 1; The duration field has been filled in with a 1 day? estimate; The task start date and finish date have been filled in using the project start date; The Gantt Chart contains a task bar representing the task; and the active cell is automatically shifted to the next row.

Activity 2-4

2. **What are the screen changes that have occurred as a result of entering the task duration?**

   The following changes have occurred: The task start and finish dates reflect the task duration, the active cell is automatically shifted to the next row, the symbol of a black diamond is displayed in the Gantt Chart for the milestone task; and the length of the task bar in the Gantt Chart increases to represent the duration.

Lesson 4

Activity 4-7

1. **Which resources are overallocated?**

   Writer 1, Editor 1, and Staff Assistant 2 are overallocated resources; these are indicated in red and by the exclamation mark in the Indicators column.

Lesson 5

Activity 5-2

4. **Why aren't we adding more resources to non-critical tasks?**

    Adding additional resources to non-critical tasks would not affect the project finish date.

Activity 5-3

3. **Why hasn't the project finish date changed to reflect the task division?**

    The task relationship that exists between Tasks 12 and 13 is a finish-to-start relationship. It needs to be changed to a start-to-start relationship.

Glossary

base calendars

A template that is used to schedule the standard working and non-working time for a set of resources.

Baselines

Original project plans used to monitor a project's progress.

Budget resource

The maximum capacity for a project to consume money, work, or material units.

combination view

A view that displays two views, with the view in the bottom pane showing detailed information about the data selected in the top pane.

Constraints

Conditions or limitations placed on the start or finish date of a task in a project plan.

Cost resource

The miscellaneous expenses that vary from task to task and independent of the amount of work performed on the task.

critical path

The series of tasks that determines the calculated start date or finish date of the project.

critical tasks

The tasks on the critical path.

Deadline

A target date indicating when you want a task to be completed.

Duration

The time interval between the start and end time of a task.

field

A location in a sheet, form, or chart that contains a specific kind of information about a task, resource, or assignment.

Lag Time

A delay between two dependent tasks.

Lead Time

The overlap between two tasks that are linked by a dependency.

leveling

The process of delaying or splitting tasks to resolve conflicts.

Material resource

The supplies or other consumable items used to complete tasks in a project.

milestone

A task with a zero duration that acts as a reference point marking a major project event.

Outlining

Process of creating a hierarchical structure in a project that shows how tasks can be delegated to various levels.

overallocated resource

A resource that's scheduled to work beyond its capacity.

part-time resource

A resource scheduled to work less than 40 hours in a work week.

Project calendar

The base calendar that specifies the default working and non-working times for a project.

Project Guide

A tool that provides detailed instructions and controls to help you build and manage your projects.

Project summary task

The highest level of work in a project that represents the project goal or project objective.

recurring task

A task that occurs repeatedly at regular intervals during the course of a project.

report

A format for generating project information that is appropriate for distribution.

Resource calendar

A calendar created to specify working and non-working times for an individual resource when exceptions from the base calendar exist.

Resources

The people, equipment, material, and other miscellaneous items used to complete the tasks.

Slack

The amount of time that a task can slip before it affects another task or the project's finish date.

Subtask

Task that contain the detailed steps necessary to complete summary tasks that are represented in the Gantt Chart by blue bars.

Summary task

Task that contain the broad concepts of projects that are represented in the Gantt Chart by black bars with black triangular terminators.

tables

A format that displays different fields of data for tasks and resources within a sheet view.

Task calendar

A calendar applied to an individual task created to control the scheduling of a task when exceptions from the base calendar exist.

Task Drivers Pane

A pane that provides information on factors affecting the start date of the selected tasks and enables easy browsing of the critical path in a project plan.

Task notes

Additional or supporting information that is added to a task.

task

Is an individual work item that defines a piece of work required to complete a project.

unit

The representation of the percentage of a resource's time assigned to a task.

Work Breakdown Structure

A hierarchy of tasks in a project represented by alphanumeric codes that identify each task's unique place in the structure.

Work resource

The people or equipment used to complete tasks in a project.

Work

The total amount of person-hours required to complete the resource's assignment.

Index